GRANDPARENTS' RIGHTS

What Every Grandparent Needs to Know

By

Patricia Perkins Slorah, Ph.D.

This book is a work of nonfiction, however names and places have been changed to protect identities. Any resemblance to actual persons, living or dead, is coincidental.

ISBN: 1-4107-6628-4 (e-book)
ISBN: 1-4107-6627-6 (Paperback)

Library of Congress Control Number: 2003094649

This book is printed on acid free paper.

Printed in the United States of America
Bloomington, IN

1stBooks - rev. 07/22/03

TABLE OF CONTENTS

FOREWARD

If you are reading this book, the chances are very good that you are - or know someone who is - concerned about a situation requiring grandparents' rights. Because I have been personally involved in the subject since 1988, I understand your need for information. In Chapter 2 you will read my story. My purpose in writing this book is to provide you with the facts I learned, when I was in the throes of despair over this very misunderstood issue.

My professional involvement began while I was working toward my doctorate in anthropology at the University of South Florida in Tampa. During my course of study I presented a report based on Dr. Arthur Kornhaber's research. Dr. Kornhaber, a child psychiatrist, specializing in at-risk children studies conflict between grandparents and parents.

I also introduced the idea of grandparents' legal rights, a concept previously unknown to everyone in the class. After I had presented my report, every hand in the room shot up.

Literally everyone was interested, and had questions about what I had presented. At the end of the evening, the professor announced to the class that I had found the research subject for my doctoral work in Applied Anthropology. This was news to me, but proved to be a serendipitous pronouncement.

At that time I knew absolutely no one (except our family) who had the same problem, however, that was to change drastically. In 1994 I was granted a doctorate degree based on my work in this area, and the following year was made a Fellow in the Society for Applied Anthropology for empowering Florida grandparents to bring about sweeping changes in the Florida grandparents' rights law.

My research in this area was done under the aegis of both the Anthropology and the Gerontology Departments at the University of South Florida in Tampa. The Department of Aging and Mental Health of the Florida Mental Health Institute on the Tampa campus of the university also assisted for one year by graciously providing me with an office and an assistant.

Although I am no longer active in support group activities, I wrote this book with the hope it will answer questions and provide comfort to grandparents, who have become estranged from beloved grandchildren.

I would like to thank my husband, Jack, for his patience and diligence in helping me write this book. Without my wonderful and loving friend, Barb, I would never have finished it. I cannot ever fully repay her for the hours she spent editing and making insightful suggestions. Sally Schenk gave generously of her expertise as a degreed English major and provided a polish that otherwise would have been lacking. I would also like to thank Barb's husband, Peter, and my friend and neighbor, Anastasia Seelig.

If there are any mistakes, inaccuracies, or omissions, I take full responsibility.

CHAPTER 1

OVERVIEW OF GRANDPARENTS' RIGHTS

Grandparents' rights are simply the right to petition the court for visitation with a grandchild; they do not automatically insure visitation. To obtain visitation, you must petition the court and request a judicial order stating when and under what circumstances, you may see your grandchild.

Some judges do not believe in grandparents' rights and thus may turn your petition down. In this book, however, you will read stories of grandparents who obtained court-ordered visitation. These grandparents were awarded visitation because they convinced the court that their grandchild needed their continuing presence as a stabilizing influence.

Situations in which grandparents are denied visitation by the parents usually occur because of difficulties between the grandparent and the child's custodial parent. I have written this book to help you overcome these difficulties without spending a great deal of money on legal fees. *In fact, those grandparents who spend large sums of money to obtain visitation are less likely to be successful than those who spend little or nothing.*

Many grandparents wonder why they may need a court order. Often they ask, "Why do I have to go through this legal maze to acquire rights, which the law says I am entitled to?" While most state laws spell out in which situations visitation petitions are accepted, they do not explain the steps necessary to obtain visitation. After reading this book, you will have the information you need to make informed decisions about your particular situation.

Prior to 1970 those grandparents who needed legal intervention to retain ties with grandchildren were out of luck, because there were no grandparents' rights laws. Since then, state laws have been enacted largely due to the efforts of grandparents who lobbied legislators in their behalf; we are fortunate indeed that others made this sacrifice.

There is a common misconception that grandparents who seek court-ordered visitation are trouble makers and that may be true in some instances, although that has not been my experience. The overwhelming majority of grandparents (and there have been thousands) who contact me, are worried that their grandchildren are being abused or neglected. Unfortunately, in far too many cases, they are correct.

The Heart of the Issue of Grandparents' Rights

The real issue of grandparents' rights is protection of a parent-like bond that is formed as a result of extensive involvement with caregiving. Most likely, nothing in our life has prepared us for the turmoil into which we are thrust when we assume responsibility for our distressed grandchildren.

We know children fare best when they live in an atmosphere where conflicts are worked out through reasonable discussion. The best-adjusted child is one who knows what to expect, has rules, family dinners, and parents who get along with each other as well as with extended family, neighbors, teachers, and law enforcement officers. Children will become what they learn; if parents teach them disrespect, they will become disrespectful.

However, from the perspective of the parents, the issue of grandparents' rights is merely a way for overbearing grandparents to legally interfere in their God-given right as parents. That may be true in isolated cases, but in my experience that is far from the norm.

As a member of the grandparent generation, I now believe we misled our daughters. We told them that because of new attitudes toward women, they could 'have it all.' We neglected to tell them they could not 'have it all at once.'

As you will read throughout this book, there are many challenges to adequate parenting in our modern world. Some of these are:

- Divorce
- Fierce competition in the job market
- Lack of quality daycare
- Financial problems
- Substance abuse.

As grandparents who care, we learn that when parents do not live in accordance with the rules of a civilized society, children turn to those on whom they have come to depend. As a grandparent you may have been called in the middle of the night by neighbors, police, or acquaintances because your grandchild was in danger. Some of us may have come to expect such situations, while our adult children or involved in-laws deny the seriousness of the matter and the harm to which our grandchildren are being exposed.

CHAPTER 2

PERSONAL EXPERIENCE WITH GRANDPARENTS' RIGHTS

My introduction to grandparents' rights began when our daughter was going through a devastating divorce and beginning to date. It appeared to me that she was putting her social life before the welfare of her daughter.

Although I would like to tell you that I voiced my concerns quietly and calmly, that was not the case. I did all the wrong things. I became very angry and yelled a lot. At one point my daughter asked if I thought she was a good mother. I, unfortunately, answered rather bluntly which precipitated our being cut off from our grandchild.

I felt shame when friends and extended family found out that my husband and I had been denied visitation and had to sue our daughter to see our granddaughter. Many believed, and conveyed the belief, that I must be somehow to blame. They conveyed their skepticism in a number of ways; some subtle, others not so subtle – either way, it hurt.

Some asked, "What did you do to your daughter to make her so angry at you?" Others offered unsolicited advice such as, "You know you have to let go and let her make her own mistakes." Unfortunately, such mistakes can result in permanent damage or death to a child involved.

I was deeply troubled by our situation, worried about our grandchild, and hurt by what I perceived to be a lack of caring, by society, toward children who are risk of abuse and neglect. Indifference seemed to be especially entrenched in the social service fields.

Never did I imagine that I would publicly reveal information about a deeply troubling personal heartache. Yet, I did so because I knew it was the only way in which I would be able to find the cause of the problem and help myself and the myriad other grandparents in the same situation. Research confirmed that child maltreatment is not confined to people who live chaotic lives; it became very evident that this problem is occurring as a part of every day middle-class life.

To tell my story on television, to have it written in newspapers across the country, to testify before the United States House of Representative's Special Committee on Aging, were things that were initially unthinkable to me. But that is exactly what I eventually did.

A Guiding Force

Fortunately, when the problem began I sought help the way I have always done – I looked for a book to provide insight into the problem. It was at this point that I found Dr. Kornhaber's book, *Between Parents and Grandparents*.

I liked what I read and I called Dr. Kornhaber who spoke with me briefly giving me several extremely helpful recommendations. He suggested I contact Lucille Sumpter, a grandmother in Michigan, who had launched practically every grandparent support group in the United States.

Dr. Kornhaber also suggested I obtain a book published by the American Bar Association (ABA) on grandparents' rights. This wonderful paperback (which is unfortunately no longer in print) provided guidelines for judges, lawyers, and mediators involved in grandparent visitation cases. The ABA book provided invaluable inside information, which helped not only me but thousands of other grandparents in the same situation.

Lucille Sumpter convinced me of the need to start a support group, to meet my own emotional needs as well as those of many other grandparents in Florida who had contacted her.

Counseling Helped Initially

My husband, daughter, her new husband, and I began seeing a counselor, 'Billie,' who related privately that she had lived both sides

9

of the issue of child maltreatment. She remarried after divorcing a man with many problems only to find herself encumbered with a substance abuser. Billie's efforts to control his drinking resulted in neglect of her children and brought about rancor between Billie and her mother.

Billie told me if her mother "had not bought the children's clothing they would not have had any." Billie's children grew up and became poor parents; eventually Billie discovered her grandchildren had been taken from their parents and placed in foster care. She located them in California only to find the oldest granddaughter pregnant. Since Billie refused to rear the child and the girl was not old enough to care for the baby, Billie's first great-grandchild was placed for adoption. This fact greatly distressed Billie and was a major factor in her choice of work as a counselor for child abuse prevention.

Billie had great empathy and easily worked with both parents and grandparents. She convinced our daughter and new son-in-law to work on marital and parenting issues with another counselor in the same office. Billie worked with my husband and me as well as with our five-year-old granddaughter, whom she introduced into a group for children at risk for abuse and neglect. Things began to improve until Billie became ill and died within a very short time.

The counselor (Doris) who took Billie's place was ill-prepared to do so, and had been counseling our daughter and son-in-law in both marriage and parenting skills. Doris believed her greatest counseling strong point was the fact that she had been married and divorced five times. After Billie's death, Doris turned against my husband and me and eventually our daughter no longer allowed us to see our granddaughter. I believe she thought we were planning to seek custody of our granddaughter, since other women in the parenting group had lost custody of their children to either their own mother or their former husband.

Court was Last Resort

We went to an attorney only after everything else failed. We tried to resolve things out of court with a letter - hand carried to our daughter laying out the issues and our desire to resolve them. Nothing happened for a month. Meanwhile I was worried sick about our little granddaughter, who was now without the love and support I had given her.

We asked our lawyer to get a court date, which she promptly did. Two weeks later, along with our daughter, we stood in front of a judge at four o'clock on a Friday afternoon. The judge ordered us all to mediation and said we would be permitted to begin temporary visitation in two days – on Sunday morning. We were extremely lucky.

Mediation

Mediation lasted from June through December and was held in a small dingy office building in the courthouse complex. We were searched for weapons (in front of others present in the waiting room) and an armed bailiff sat in the room during every mediation session. Each of us filled out a form giving date of birth, job status, level of education, and other verifiable information.

The mediator, who chewed on a toothpick all during our sessions, seemed to take issue with my educational level. He asked in what field my degrees were and seemed especially antagonistic toward me in the way he phrased questions and in the statements he made. Having read the ABA book I knew not to react. He seemed to be stymied until our granddaughter's father was allowed into the mediation.

Our granddaughter's natural father said he had no problem with our seeing our granddaughter, but that he had a problem with his own visitation with her. He requested her attendance at her half-sister's birthday, which was on a day that he did not have visitation. Things got tense. The mediator decided that perhaps the problem was not with me after all.

That was the last mediation session we had. We all agreed on the terms of visitation and the mediator included a statement in the court order that both the parents and the grandparents sit down once a month and discuss pertinent childrearing issues. It was a show of confidence in us that this paragraph was included; however, we were never involved in discussing anything. We were simply left to "pick up the pieces."

There have been many ups and downs since then, but we have resolved our differences to the point that I was asked to be present at our grandson's birth several years later and we also continue to enjoy family dinners on special occasions.

Benefits of Perseverance

Today this same granddaughter, with whom we sought visitation, has lived in our home for three years. She is a young woman with a responsible job and a baby to whom she is a wonderful parent. She goes to college at night and has a 4.0 average. We are very proud of her and enjoy seeing both of them every single day.

CHAPTER 3

GRANDPARENT SUPPORT GROUPS

When separated from a grandchild, we need rapport with others who are grappling with this very difficult situation. A grandparent support group can be invaluable; however, such groups are likely to be scarce for several reasons; 1) They tend to be emotionally draining and thus hard on the leader, 2) They are short-lived because of the aims of those who attend them.

Grandparents who attend support group meetings tend to fall into one of two categories: 1) One group lacks the will to make the sacrifices necessary to achieve visitation. They usually attend only a few meetings and tend to be either very quiet or very argumentative about the difficult process of obtaining visitation

2) Those in the second category are willing to do whatever it takes to remain connected to their grandchildren. These grandparents usually are successful but quit attending the

group because they become so busy with their grandchildren!

Perhaps you wish to start your own support group. This chapter will give you a general idea of what benefits you can reasonably expect, as well as some of the guidelines that are needed for successful groups.

Emotional Support

The biggest relief grandparents at the support group realize is the knowledge that they are not alone in their struggle. Those who are grappling with the intense pain of being cut off from a beloved grandchild feel a common bond with others in this situation. It doesn't matter if there are wide economic and cultural differences; empathy knows no boundaries.

Patricia Perkins Slorah, Ph.D.

Information

Grandparents can obtain recommendations for attorneys, where to find second-hand clothing stores for children, ways to find parents who have fled, how to file petitions for visitation and information on the latest grandparent visitation legislation. Remember, anyone can start a support group. *Worthwhile support groups are those in which you hear the stories of grandparents who have won visitation with grandchildren.*

This chapter will provide you with some important dos and don'ts about grandparent support groups.

Do:

• Find at least one other person who will help you. That individual does not have to be a grandparent without visitation, but must be someone who is sympathetic to the cause of grandparents' rights.

• Locate a public place that will not charge you a fee for a room. Libraries, hospitals, and

18

churches are good places to look because they will advertise your group in their newsletter.

• Determine how often you want to meet and what time of day. If a majority of working people attend, then you will need to meet in the evening or on Saturday. If many older people attend, they may not want to drive at night and would prefer daytime meetings.

• Decide if you want to have dues, a one-time fee, or voluntary donations. If you meet in a public place, you will not be able to stipulate that individuals must pay dues in order to attend. However, you will need money for copying costs, for postage, for refreshments, or for holding special events. Some groups have a basket they pass at the end of the meeting for donations.

• Designate a chairperson to start and end the meeting. This person will need to control who talks and how long so that each person attending has a chance to talk if he or she wishes to do so. Try to keep meetings to an hour.

• Place a notice each month in the paper to advertise the time, place and date of the meeting. A contact person's telephone number should also be listed.

• Pass around a sheet of paper at each meeting requesting that those who desire to be called or notified by mail of the next meeting include their telephone number or address.

• Hand out clothes pins to remind grandparents to 'hang in there.' We also gave them to those who had a tendency to be critical of parents and told them to 'apply to lips as needed.'

Because of the nature of the discussions, it is unwise for anyone other than a grandparent with a problem to attend.

The news media can play a critical role in making grandparents aware that the support group exists, as well as provide publicity to grandparents seeking meaningful legislative change. However, only the leader of the group should be the one to choose who will speak with reporters, appear on talk radio or on television.

I knew of an instance in which a newspaper reporter was allowed to be present at a grandparent support group meeting and the results were disastrous. A large number of grandparents showed up because they "wanted to get their story out" and the leader of the group had trouble controlling them. Several people got out of hand and said things that were indiscreet, and the reporter ended up writing a very unflattering newspaper article.

It may be that you will acquire all the information you need in this book and will decide you do not wish to commit to a support group. However, keep in mind that in a group you will hear some very sobering stories. Gaining visitation with a grandchild from whom you have been cut off is a long and difficult process. It may be one of the most painful struggles of your life.

No attorney can force a judge to give you visitation with your grandchild. You are the one who will determine whether or not you are successful. Visitation laws only open the door for you; from then on it's all up to you.

While the information you read in this book is perhaps not what you want to hear, it will save you thousands of dollars (in money spent on attorneys for visitation or defense attorneys for delinquent children) if you accept it and follow the guidelines in later chapters. You may decide that it is less costly – not to mention less risky – to simply settle your differences with your grandchild's custodian without taking the matter to court.

CHAPTER 4

GRANDPARENTS AS A VOTING BLOC

Publicity is Power

As an issue, grandparents' rights are of great interest to the media. Stories complete with pictures of grandparents holding framed photographs of grandchildren or gazing longingly at empty swing sets are often picked up by the Associated Press (AP) and run in newspapers all across the country. The reason is simple; such stories sell newspapers.

The day our first support group notice appeared in newsprint, we received an invitation to appear on a major television show in the Tampa Bay area. Subsequently, requests for grandparents willing to tell their story in print or on television came pouring in. Media interest is fueled in part by the fact that older adults are a growing group of consumers.

And because politicians love publicity, they gravitate naturally toward senior groups, which they see as hotbeds of political power. Every legislator knows that while retirees are more demographically diverse than any other age group, they stand united on two issues; social security and grandparents' rights. It is political suicide to be publicly against either.

As a result of this welcome publicity, I was asked to testify before the Florida Judicial Subcommittee on Family Law. Several influential legislators with older constituents were being pressured to pass legislation favorable to grandparents with visitation problems. At the same time, there were legislators who placed themselves on certain committees for the sole purpose of blocking this legislation.

Like a little lamb being led to slaughter, I was unaware of the fierce opposition intrinsic in this issue. Thus, I was ill prepared for the reception I was about to receive. When called to the podium, I brought along documentation on what I knew about grandparents' rights. I noticed my various notebooks and journals were met with groans and rolling eyes by rude lawyers on the committee.

When told that a great many states had laws which allowed visitation petitions in intact family situations, many were incredulous. One influential legislator, from a district heavily populated by seniors, stood up and said she didn't believe it. No one on the committee knew that the ABA had published a book on the subject and were chagrined that I, in fact, had the book with me. As they rushed forward to see it, I was dismissed from the podium.

Legislators Harass Grandparents

The rudeness was not confined to my visit to Tallahassee, our state capital. After returning home I received several calls from the aides of legislators who had been bombarded with letters from grandparents demanding support for legislative change. These aides admitted they harassed grandparents who sent letters.

The aides apparently called those who sent in form letters and quizzed them about the fine points of the issue. These grandparents, the aides told me, sent "dirty, torn pieces of paper" and "didn't even understand the broader problem of grandparents' rights."

One aide said, "I've chased you all over the state; trying to find who was behind all this." At that point I knew I was home free. For one thing, the legislators felt vulnerable or they would not have gone to so much trouble. And for another, I knew I had the ammunition to fire up all the grandparents so they would work even harder. I politely informed each of the aides that behind every dirty, torn piece of paper they received, was a registered voter in their district. That always effectively ended the conversation!

Grandparents Learn to Lobby

Grandparents were initially astonished to discover that their legislators check to see if they are registered to vote before making a decision to listen to them on an issue. This is a key factor in successful lobbying for legislative change, so grandparents interested in visitation rights who had not registered to vote, immediately did so.

As the legislative session progressed, one grandparent or another would call every few days to see how 'our' bill was doing in committee. Soon legislators from all over the state were unwittingly helping to build our network of support, "GRAMPS" (Grandparents' Rights Advocacy Movement Political Segment), as one by one, they responded to pressure from grandparents in their district. They became fond of telling us that they were FOR our bill, but their colleague at one end of the state had said it would pass over his "dead body." In the next day or two, there would be somebody at the other end of the state who was against it.

Gradually we set up a network of contacts all over the state that would call a relative, a friend or an influential person in a particular district and tell them to put out the word to turn up the pressure. Older persons, who were not even personally involved, helped us out because they knew that someday they might need the law.

Grandparents went from table to table in restaurants patronized by seniors asking them to sign petitions. They also passed out form letters at grocery stores or placed them under windshield wipers in parking lots. Eventually these letters and petitions caught the attention of the legislators. No Florida state senator or representative wanted to anger a bloc of determined elder voters!

Success in Six Months

In May of 1990, just six months after organizing, grandparents had obtained concessions in Florida's law. Grandparents won the right to petition in the following cases: 1) when their grandchild was born out of wedlock and 2) when their grandchild had been taken from their parents by social services. Additionally, the term 'grandparents' was re-defined as including great-grandparents. At 4 a.m. on the last day of the legislative session; a chain of telephone calls went all over Florida as grandparents shared the joyful news of our victory.

CHAPTER 5

SOCIAL CONTEXT OF THE ISSUE

After learning that we are not alone, the next thing that makes grandparents feel better is to learn that our predicament is not all our fault. While we certainly did not make the situation better by trying to change an adult's behavior, a great load is lifted from our shoulders as we realize that the problem in part is one born of societal change. Let's look at some of the changes that have occurred in the past century.

Societal Changes

Grandparents are Healthier. The age at which people become grandparents has remained somewhat constant over the last century, but the amount of time a person spends as a grandparent has greatly expanded. What this means for grandchildren is that they stand a much greater chance of getting to know several of their grandparents, and will remain in contact with some of them as adults.

Increased life expectancy and better health of older adults has meant that grandparents are increasingly available to provide caregiving assistance to working mothers with young children. Many grandparents are even providing a home for their grandchildren. However, American society has not yet recognized that since grandparents are providing enormous benefits both to young parents and their offspring, there is a greater need for dependable, consistent legal protection.

Working Mothers. Today, many young mothers find it necessary to work, either to add to their husband's income, or as the sole support of their families. Some women work to protect their independence, and increasing numbers of mothers are regarding employment as a career, rather than as a supplement to the household's income.

Working mothers face many difficulties including;

- lack of parental leave to care for sick children,
- long work hours,
- the high cost of day care,
- the burden of housework and cooking after a long day of work outside the home.

Long work hours are hard on young mothers in several other ways. They make it difficult to provide supervision and transportation for children and difficult to provide a nurturing home environment.

After putting in a full day's work, an exhausted mother must then prepare a meal for cranky, hungry children. No wonder the harried mother is tempted to allow the television set to entertain the children so she has a few minutes peace after a long day.

In addition to requiring strict adherence to drop-off and pick-up hours, licensed day care centers are expensive. In Florida, the average current rate for one child is eight thousand dollars ($8,000) a year. Therefore, many single mothers must rely on sub-standard care or press grandparents into full-service babysitting.

While mothers work, grandparents are often asked to collect sick grandchildren from school or day care or take them for doctor's visits and pick up needed prescriptions. Additionally, many grandparents pay the medical bills.

When grandparents provide full-time daycare, mothers stand a better chance of being promoted because they are more relaxed and can better concentrate on their career duties without worrying about whether their children are being cared for properly. And, very often, grandparents feed, bathe, and get their grandchildren ready for bed before their mothers pick them up.

Stresses on Grandparents As Caregivers

Do most grandparents expect to rear another generation? No, not usually and given a choice, most of us would prefer not to. But that is exactly what we are doing - in increasingly greater numbers.

Children at Risk. If you are not a grandparent in such a situation, you may be asking why anyone would take on such a task. Grandparents do so – some at considerable sacrifice – for the sake of their grandchildren. We are afraid that grandchildren will not be cared for properly without our help.

The Cost of Caring. Grandparents who provide extensive care may suffer physically, financially, and emotionally. Childcare is physically demanding. Many older women suffer from osteoporosis or arthritis in addition to cardiovascular problems. Looking after active youngsters takes a toll on already diminished energy levels.

Sacrifices. When one sees that a grandchild needs clothing, shoes, or medical care, grandmothers with meager incomes quite often put these requirements ahead of their own medical needs. That sometimes means putting off doctor's visits and not filling their own expensive prescriptions.

Peers Don't Understand. A spouse or friend, who wants to enjoy the company of a grandparent, may advise them to "just say no." But grandparents cannot turn their back on grandchildren who may be at risk for abuse or neglect.

As older adults, we need friends to help us adjust to the many changes that occur in later life. However, because of concern for grandchildren, caregiving grandparents may feel isolated and lonely. Those of us who provide a great deal of care for grandchildren are often surprised that we do not receive emotional support from our peers for our sacrifices.

The phenomenon of grandparents providing extensive care for grandchildren is relatively new, and many people – including professionals – may view us as being the cause of our own problems.

Historical Differences in Family Roles

Neither of my grandmothers ever babysat for me or my siblings. My maternal grandmother was still producing offspring when her daughters were having children. When she reached my age, she looked easily twenty years older than either I or my friends. She was in poor health and had no income of her own. Since my grandfather was a veterinarian, and self-employed, she was not entitled to social security.

My grandmother was born toward the end of the 19th century, my mother at the beginning of the 20th century, and I was born toward the middle of the 20th century. Instead of providing resources to the next generation – as is often the case now - my grandmother's children provided for her as she aged.

Children as Resources. My maternal grandparents had nine children, six of whom survived to adulthood. At that time, children were useful as labor. They helped with younger children and with housework; when they were older they contributed the money they earned at outside jobs toward the household income.

Children as Liabilities. Today, such wage-earning roles for children are considered inappropriate. Currently children are economic liabilities, rather than economic assets. Their liability has increased as more and more young mothers join the work force. Issues that caregiving grandparents are presently experiencing are part of the cultural adaptations that emerge as social change occurs. These cultural adaptations are not yet widely recognized by society as a whole, and therein lies the problem. In the next chapter, we will examine the impact on our grandchildren.

CHAPTER 6

A PATTERN EMERGES

As people began to attend our monthly grandparent support group meetings, I was amazed to hear how similar the stories were. Although we came from all walks of life, a pattern emerged quickly as we shared our experiences. It became clear that the majority of us were dealing with very serious issues.

Troubled Families

Almost none of the grandchildren, discussed at support group meeting, resided in a family where biological parents still lived together. Several of the grandparents had lost adult children due to unexpected death. A few had adult children who became parents out of wedlock. Many had children who were divorced. Several had children who remained married, but abuse was occurring within the family due to a variety of stressors.

Financial woes, substance abuse, and problems with the law were common themes discussed in support group meetings. Sometimes grandparents would start to tell their story, only to be interrupted by another group member who offered to tell the rest of the narrative. No one had trouble identifying with the terrible stories told in those meetings.

The accounts of abuse were so appalling that almost every support group meeting was a wrenching experience - people cried at the meetings; some left because they were sickened with grief.

The meetings went on for several hours as participants poured out concerns for their grandchildren. Very often despite the length of the meetings, many people would stay afterward to talk privately. It was emotionally draining for everyone.

At-Risk Children

Grandparents graphically related the types of abuse their grandchildren were suffering. Most common was neglect followed by physical abuse, and emotional mistreatment. We learned that sexual abuse is the most difficult type of maltreatment with which grandparents have to cope because of the stigma attached. Mothers are most likely to be neglectful while husband and boyfriends are most likely to be involved in physical or sexual abuse. Mothers often will not admit that their boyfriend/husband has committed such an offense, and become angry when the allegation is made.

Over time we learned that there are several kinds of abuse, for example emotional abuse is likely when caregiving grandparents are separated from grandchildren with whom they have previously had a loving relationship. The grandchildren believe they are somehow at fault; that their grandparents abandoned them because they are 'bad.' Several grandparents related that upon seeing their grandchild for the first time after obtaining court-ordered visitation, the first thing the child said was, "Please let me come home. I'll be good."

Several grandparents reported that their daughter cared for one child better (though still not adequately) than another. Research indicates that usually the first child is most neglected because the mother was clearly not mature enough to bond with this baby. Other grandparents told how their daughter or in-law would leave their grandbaby with 'just anybody' so she could go out and party.

Exposure to marital violence is considered emotional abuse because children who witness such disturbances are likely as adults to either become abusive or to allow themselves to become victims of abuse. Such behavior exposes children to a dysfunctional link between love and violence which serves to legitimize violence in the family.

Physical Abuse. This type of abuse usually occurs because the caregiver wants to force the child to do something of which he or she is incapable, thereby inflicting severe or mortal physical damage on the child. WARNING: The mother's boyfriend is twenty-seven (27) times more likely to physically abuse a child than any other caregiver.

Boyfriends may become physically abusive when they try to assert parental authority, which older children do not believe they possess. Children may say, "Who are you to tell me what to do? You're not my father." The boyfriend, incensed, may reply, "I'll show you who I am!"

Very young babies may be shaken to make them stop crying; toddlers being potty-trained are at risk for burns in a very hot bathtub or for being drowned in the toilet. Parents most likely to perpetrate this abuse often are emotionally immature, substance abusers with financial and relationship problems.

I remember specifically one couple who came to some of the support group meetings. At the first meeting they revealed their concern about the safety of their grandson. At a subsequent meeting, when I asked them to fill out a questionnaire on a study I was conducting they left blank the answer to the question, "Do you think your grandchild is being abused?"

They did not attend meetings for several months, but later told the group their grandson had been severely beaten by the mother's boyfriend. The child's injuries were discovered when the mother dropped him off for visitation. The grandparents immediately took him to the emergency room at the hospital where the attending physician called the police. After his hospitalization, they brought their grandson home in a full body cast.

The grandparents were given custody of their grandchild while he recovered from his injuries. During this time, they discovered he was malnourished and that he had never once been to a dentist. His grandmother reported they needed to spend several thousand dollars on dental care for him.

Later when the child was returned to his mother, the grandparents were forced to pay an attorney in order to obtain visitation rights even though they (the grandparents) had been given custody of the child by the State.

These same grandparents had voiced concerns in the group prior to filling out the questionnaire, and later reported evidence that their grandchildren were being maltreated.

Why hadn't these grandparents answered the study question about whether or not they believed their grandchild was being abused or neglected? My guess is that they were too anxious. Or perhaps they were indulging in wishful thinking as was the case with several grandparents who answered only, "I hope not" or "I don't know" thus further endangering their grandchild.

Neglect. Such maltreatment is defined as failure to provide adequately for the child when clearly able to do so. Parental ignorance or poverty is not considered neglect because it does not involve intent.

Many of the mothers who neglect their children do so because they are irresponsible, while others have definable reasons such as substance abuse problems. Some may have become pregnant without means of supporting the children they bear. In such cases they may turn the children over to their own mother to rear, but retain the right to make all decisions concerning the child's welfare.

A number of grandparent caregivers suffer financial deprivation, despite the fact that the State or the father is providing support money. It is common practice for mothers to tell grandparent caregivers that they will allow them to take care of their grandchildren as long as they give the mother any support money that is intended for the grandchildren.

In many such cases, support money is actually controlled by the mother's boyfriend. In situations like this, grandchildren are used as pawns. For example, a parent tells grandparents, "You can see them only if you buy their clothes, or their Christmas presents, or don't report me to the Department of Children and Families," and so forth.

Margaret's Story

I include Margaret Chesterton's story here as an extreme example of neglect, substance abuse, and the inability of the social service system to handle many problems with which they are confronted. I am not blaming the "system" for this, but clearly Margaret needed help for herself and her grandchildren, and it was not forthcoming.

I interviewed Margaret in the kitchen of her small home in an older section of one of the larger cities in the central west coast area of Florida. She had prepared lunch for us and we sat at the table for quite a while as I took notes and tape recorded Margaret as she told her story. Margaret is a middle-aged woman whose face is lined with fatigue and gives the appearance of someone who has had to deal with many adversities in her adult life.

Margaret is worn out from her hard life. Her former husband, who was an alcoholic, became homeless and was later found dead on the street in a northern city, leaving Margaret the responsibility of rearing their three children alone.

I have known Margaret since 1991, when she came to the group asking how to obtain court-ordered visitation. She was seeking relief from her daughter's incessant demands, capitulation to which always preceded Margaret's being able to spend time with her then six-year-old granddaughter, whom she had reared. At this time there was another child, a baby with whom Margaret was steadfastly refusing to bond in order to avoid further heartbreak.

I was able to give Margaret the name of an attorney associated with our group who provided his services to her without charge. She was disappointed with the results of the court hearing, however, because instead of granting her regular court-ordered visitation, the judge remanded Margaret and her daughter to counseling.

Margaret resisted the advice of her attorney and stubbornly refused both to include the baby in the visitation and to go to counseling. Therefore, she was forced to see her granddaughter at the convenience of the mother (Margaret's daughter). Jocelyn, Margaret's daughter, allows her mother to see Celeste, but only if she spends equal time with Montgomery, the baby.

Margaret continues to lament the fact that the hearing was devastating to her and that she will never get over it, and is particularly worn down with the many trials she has had to endure because of her youngest daughter, Jocelyn. Her two older children have successful lives and marriages, but her youngest daughter has caused Margaret untold grief.

Over the years Jocelyn has been addicted to alcohol and to crank, a methamphetamine sometimes used by bikers. She dropped out of high school and from time to time has worked as a topless dancer and stripper to support herself. As a teenager she ran away a number of times and at one time was involved in a scheme to murder her mother in order to sell Margaret's car for drug money. Her boyfriend at the time, a motorcycle gang member, is currently serving time in prison for the foiled scheme.

Jocelyn gave birth out-of-wedlock several times. For a number of years, she was able to live independently of Margaret because she received Aid to Families with Dependent Children, food stamps, a housing allowance, and Medicaid. Margaret reports that Jocelyn's stream of boyfriends are partially attracted by her income and housing. Margaret bought Jocelyn a used car one year so she could get back and forth to work. However, her current boyfriend talked her into trading it on another one that he put in both their names.

Margaret reports that many times she has been called by neighbors in the middle of the night to come for Celeste because Jocelyn was fighting with her current boyfriend and they were afraid for Celeste's safety. While Jocelyn sometimes provides for her children, she cannot be depended upon to do so on a regular basis so Margaret always has to be ready to step in at a moment's notice.

Even though Margaret is hard-pressed financially, Celeste comes to her for school clothes and other necessities which are covered by welfare. If Margaret didn't provide for Celeste's and Montgomery's needs, they would go without. Margaret sees the children as often as she is able to accede to her daughter's demands.

The last time I heard from Margaret, she reported that Jocelyn had finally been sent to prison where, in Margaret's opinion, she belongs. There were multiple charges against her and she finally had to pay her debt to society. Both children are now teenagers and are more than Margaret can handle. Her grandson, Montgomery, is in foster care and, in our last telephone conversation Margaret confided that she can no longer tolerate Celeste's behavior and is planning to turn her over to the social service system. When I started writing this book, I tried to locate Margaret but was unable to do so.

Sex Abuse. Such abuse is defined as sexual activity that the child is powerless to stop. It is the betrayal by the child's caregiver, and the related social stigma, that causes irreparable damage. Improper touching, rape, child prostitution and/or child pornography are some of the inappropriate behaviors included in this category. Isolated families, male domination, and female sexual shame can spawn this type of abuse.

One member of the support group was told by her three-year old granddaughter that she was hurt by her mother's boyfriend. This grandmother called the sheriff's department and was given custody of the child and her younger brother at three o'clock one morning. She described her shock, and related how difficult it was for her to deal with this sudden responsibility while working full-time.

The mother of these children was furious and denied that her boyfriend would do such a thing. She retaliated against the grandparents by registering a physical abuse complaint. The sheriff's department investigating the complaint arrived in a marked car with the red light going so all the neighbors in the quiet neighborhood were alerted to the grandparents' humiliation.

Then a child protective service worker came to strip the children and look them over for bruises. Finding nothing, the professionals left, leaving the grandparents wondering what would happen next. Feeling very threatened, they felt they had no choice but to place the children into foster care. Sadly, these grandparents lost all contact with the children when their foster parents adopted them. The grandmother, especially, suffered great stress over the situation.

Why are such indignities to our grandchildren tolerated in American society? How can government agencies be so powerless or reluctant to protect at-risk children? In the next chapter we will examine American values that are associated with staggering statistics of child abuse and neglect in our society.

CHAPTER 7

CULTURAL VALUES AND CHILD MALTREATMENT

According to noted researcher, Jill Korbin, child abuse in American society is related to several key cultural values. First, is Western societies' value of competitive and violent behavior. Second, is denial of the existence of widespread child maltreatment. Third, is the protection of privacy, which prevents collective responsibility of children; subsumed in this value is the lack of parental intent to inflict fatal injuries - such injuries occur because of lack of intervention. Fourth, is the widespread under-valuing of children, in and of, themselves.

Violence. Although some professionals in the past have espoused expressing aggression to relieve frustration, evidence now shows that aggression provides a model of violence. Researchers have found that children who watch violent television programs are more likely to exhibit aggressive behavior than children whose television viewing is closely monitored by parents. In addition, bullying, which has long been tolerated in American secondary schools is now associated with school massacres.

The most common cause of death in children in this country is homicide. Yet, child abuse and neglect is rarely studied by researchers. What is the reason? Is it because the subject is less valued than concerns viewed as likely to impact mainstream Americans?

Denial. Denial of abuse is a common reaction in both professionals and parents. According to Korbin's research, 25% of the fatalities she studied occurred in families who were known by professionals. Forty percent (40%) of fatalities occurred shortly after the abusing parent was seen by a physician or psychiatrist. The critical component in these deaths was denial by the offending mothers and professionals, who incorrectly diagnosed the problem.

Another researcher, Leslie Margolin, studied child abuse by the mother's boyfriend. She found that mothers were particularly likely to deny that their boyfriends abused their children. Even when the live-in was convicted for fatally abusing children, mothers still refused to face the truth.

Privacy. Legislators do not like to enact legislation that allows governmental intrusion into family life. Younger constituents, particularly, do not want it. American society values parental privacy, and therefore, assumes very little collective responsibility for children's welfare.

Across cultures, children, who do not have a network of individuals concerned about their welfare, are at increased risk for maltreatment. When child rearing is a group concern, others can intercede before serious harm is done.

Lack of Intent. Parents are the perpetrators in the majority of cases of infanticide and death – but parents don't usually intend to kill their children. Death of the child is largely an unexpected, unintended, and undesired consequence of punishment.

Fatally-abusing parents do not appear markedly different from non-fatally abusing parents. All the women in Jill Korbin's study of fatally abusing mothers had previously abused their children, and some had even shown the injuries to people close to them. Undeniably these women had many problems, but no one, either friend or authority reported them or intervened to stop the abuse before it was too late.

In another study, Korbin found that the re-unification period (when children, who had been previously removed from their home, were returned by authorities) was a particularly dangerous time. Several of the children in the study were killed within weeks or months after being reunited with their mothers.

During the time I have been studying this issue, I have noticed a trend toward re-unification around holiday times. Substance abuse and feelings of financial deprivation are apt to be particularly acute at this time. Families - already at risk - are under increased pressure when a child is returned after an enforced absence.

Undervalued Children. Love aside, in a farming society, children are valued because they are economically useful. As mentioned previously, in our society today children are economic liabilities. Currently, in the Western world there is a preoccupation with materialism, so needs of children are pitted against the desires of the parents to acquire material possessions. Purchasing high-status merchandise and acquiring the rank of parenthood bring prestige to young adults, yet those who try to fulfill both of these desires at the same time are in a no-win situation. They are likely to become mired in financial disaster with each parent blaming the other for excessive spending and secretly resenting the children for their demands.

Children are valued in many cultures and, in most, extended family members and neighbors have a tacit right to intervene in matters of concern. In such societies, the value of children supercedes the status of motherhood. In American society, the status of motherhood and the value of privacy appear to supercede the safety of children.

What is the Solution?

Problems that lead to child abuse can be solved many times by providing enough support to balance the stress under which parents find themselves. Grandparents are the obvious answer to this dilemma. To protect themselves, however, adequate legislation is needed to protect the rights of both grandparents AND grandchildren, since grandparents' rights are really children's rights. As all grandparents who have become active in the grandparents' rights movement know, - the issue is called "Grandparents' Rights" for political reasons. Children don't vote, and seniors DO have political clout.

Social Change is Needed. Modern American society as a whole has a stake in promoting interdependence between generations. The research of Maria Vesperi and Jay Sokolovsky found that both the very young and the very old benefit when their needs are met by a combination of family and social services.

Laws are needed to protect the rights of caregiving grandparents, not only from a humanitarian point of view, but also to keep families, social services, and society as a whole from becoming overburdened.

Individual needs are best met by families because they do not have to accede to the myriad rules under which governmental agencies operate. Cost is minimal and reciprocal. Grandparents, who provide childcare for grandchildren from birth, form solid bonds with these children on whom they may depend later in life.

Maintaining Generational Bonds Benefits Society

Due to better health care, persons are living longer than ever before. Those who live long enough often need assistance with tasks of daily living such as bill paying, shopping, housekeeping, and even personal care. Such seniors may not be able to call upon their own children, who may be too old to provide these services without jeopardizing their own well-being.

Close bonds with grandchildren have the potential to keep seniors out of nursing homes until the last few months of their life. Because an ever-larger number of nursing homes are subsidized by government agencies, as our society ages it becomes increasingly important to keep those costs from spiraling and overburdening younger members of society.

In the next chapter we will examine how schisms in families can occur when American grandparents are intimately involved with the nuclear family.

CHAPTER 8

INTERGENERATIONAL CONFLICT

When intergenerational conflict emerges, it is made worse by lack of societal support for grandparents. Poor, black grandparents, who have long distrusted the legal system, turn to religion and grandparent support groups, while white, middle income grandparents, who lack an informal mediator, often look to child welfare authorities and the court system for help. Unfortunately, such formal intervention as the use of the court or social service system is seriously lacking in effectiveness.

Relying on the Court System can be Hazardous

Grandparents, who turn to the court system without being properly prepared, are at serious risk. Not only do they suffer, but so does the grandchild they seek to protect. Moreover, unscrupulous attorneys can easily take advantage of grandparents with deep pockets.

One such couple comes to mind. Little Frankie Fredrickson suffered as much from the emotional abuse that resulted from the inability of the adults in his life to resolve their differences as he did from the corporal punishment meted out by a brutal stepfather.

The Story Began when Ada and Frank Lived in New York City

Frankie became bonded with his grandparents when they cared for him on a daily basis so that his working parents would not have to pay for day care. Ada Fredrickson contacted me in 1991 for information about grandparent support groups in the Orlando area and we met for coffee at a local pancake house.

Ada is a short, vivacious woman who is a former college professor. Her husband, who is more reserved, is a retired insurance executive.

They went to Tallahassee from their home in Orlando and stayed throughout the entire 1993 legislative session, constantly visiting legislators and making sure that the latest grandparent rights law was not lost or cast aside.

Because of the publicity surrounding their case, I have been privy to some parts of their son's side of the story. He claimed that his parents have tried to obtain rights to his adopted son that are on an equal par with parental rights. Because of their extensive caregiving, it is reasonable to suggest that role boundaries became blurred.

Ada cared for Frankie for four years - from the day of his adoption until his parents refused to let his grandparents see Frankie any longer. It was immediately obvious that he had been well-cared for by his foster mother. She had dressed him in beautiful clothes for his new parents and even made a small book to send along, entitled, "What I Like." Inside were lists of his favorite foods, his schedule, his favorite playtimes and so forth.

Ada knew there was trouble ahead when her daughter-in-law tossed the little book in the wastebasket. Ada retrieved it and tears still come to her eyes when she recalls the love it reflected and the callousness her daughter-in-law exhibited.

The daily routine began when one of his parents would drop Frankie off early in the morning while he was still in pajamas. Ada would feed him breakfast, bathe and dress him and then would take him to one of many educational and cultural events. They were regulars at the public library story hour, where he joined with other children gathered in a circle while a story was either told or read with great animation and much audience participation. They went to the zoo, rode the train, toured art museums and attended concerts.

Ada actually resigned from her tenured position because she fell in love with the child and wanted to bring stability and love into his life. Later, their son and daughter-in-law divorced and each remarried. Ada and Frank, devout Catholics, were unhappy about their son's divorce and disapproved of the custody agreement which arranged for little Frankie (then three years old) to spend half of the week with one parent and half with the other.

Ada and Frank also did not like Frankie's stepparents. Frankie told them that his stepfather hit him and once shoved his face in his plate at the dinner table. While Frankie's stepfather admitted in court that he used corporal punishment to discipline Frankie, he claimed that he is in compliance with child protective service guidelines and does not leave welts or bruises on the child.

When Ada and Frank confronted their son about their concerns, angry words were exchanged and the result was that the Fredricksons were told that thereafter they would see Frankie only at the convenience of his parents. A lengthy and expensive legal battle took place and Ada and Frank were denied access to Frankie. They appealed the ruling and lost the appeal.

It has been nine years since the Fredricksons have seen or had any contact with their grandson. They used to mention the sadness they felt at holiday time in their yearly

Christmas cards. This past year is the first time they have not mentioned their grandson in holiday greetings.

Social Service System

Although it is quite a bit less costly than the legal system, the social service system is no more effective in handling grandparents' visitation issues. Those employed in this field, seem to have a pre-conceived notion that grandparents involved in visitation disputes are toxic and warrant little, or no, consideration.

Child Protective Workers. When I interviewed several top-ranking administrators in Child Protection Service (CPS) work, I was somewhat shocked by their attitude. One views the problem of child abuse as being that of the grandparents' making. Thomas Smithfield had this to say:

> Those disputes are invariably the result of one of two things – either the grandparent getting involved in a child custody battle with one

of their children or there being allegations of some sort of cyclical nature of abuse. The grandparents abused their children, their children are abusing their children now, and the grandparents are being denied visitation rights, or are objecting to their children's denying their access to their children because of that sort of abuse cycle.

The other CPS worker, a program director, views the "real issue underneath" is that for the grandparents "it is an opportunity to, one more time, do better than they did with their kids." She believes grandparents use the CPS to obtain custody by calling in child abuse reports in attempts to expose the parent as being unfit. The only time these reports are justified, according to these CPS workers is when the child is in immediate, extreme, physical or sexual danger.

Whether the child is clean, has appropriate clothing or nutritious food is not considered to be important in determining welfare; neither is the lifestyle of the parent an issue – the values, behaviors and associates of the parents are protected, even when clearly detrimental to the children.

When conflict occurs between parents and grandparent caregivers, there are inadequate avenues to resolve such disputes. Conflict is most likely to occur when:
• There are unclear role boundaries,
• Grandparents assume responsibility without correspondent authority, and
• There is child maltreatment by a parent, a stepparent, or a boyfriend.

Unclear Role Boundaries

When grandparents provide daily care for grandchildren, they become privy to family secrets. When it is obvious to the grandparent that the parent's behavior and values are detrimental to the child, conflict is likely to emerge.

An assertive grandparent caregiver may believe she has to step into the role of a parent and protest conditions that she views as dangerous to the child's welfare. Virtually no one in the court system or CPS will back her up in this.

Responsibility without Authority

Conflict between mothers and daughters most often occurs over who has authority over the children. Such difficulties are similar to those experienced by stepparents, because both roles lack widely accepted norms of behavior and societal support. Formal societal systems have not yet acknowledged that grandparents who care for grandchildren provide an invaluable service and should be honored and supported, rather than maligned.

Prevention of Child Maltreatment

As we discussed in a previous chapter, denial is rampant in situations of child abuse.

No parent wants to admit that their child is being abused or neglected and heated words are likely to be exchanged when the issue emerges.

Grandparents find themselves in a double bind at this juncture. If they know of abuse and do not report it, the child may be seriously injured or killed. If they do report it and the child is taken from the home, the parent has the right to dictate whether the child is to be placed with relatives. If the child is placed in foster care, the grandparents may lose all contact.

I have met grandparents whose grandchild was placed for adoption, with the stipulation that no family member could adopt the child. Why was this done? Because the child, a twin, was born with Down's syndrome and the mother did not want to be reminded of a child of hers whom she considered less than perfect. The mother in question kept the 'normal' child, and gave the other away.

Since the birth of the twins was not kept a secret, sooner or later the twin remaining with her parents will find out that she has a sister. How will this impact her relationship with her mother? Will she worry that she, too, may be given away? The mother's decision was perfectly legal and there was nothing the distraught grandmother could do about it.

Sex abuse is a particularly disturbing situation. When grandchildren confide to grandparents about this, it is almost always with the promise that it will be kept in secret. This is a promise grandparents cannot keep. The child then feels doubly betrayed and could be cut off from contact with the grandparent, if a vindictive parent requests.

Other Conflicts

Researchers found conflict to be most frequent in the group of grandparental caregivers whose adult child and grandchildren live with them. Other situations that are conflictual are those in which the grandparent provides only daycare.

Those grandparents who have formal custody of grandchildren are less likely to have problems while the custody is in place. When children are remanded to their parents, however, grandparents are frequently cut off because of feelings of anger on the part of parents.

Social service workers often are pleasant while grandparents have custody, but turn a deaf ear to the grandparent's pleas for visitation rights when reunification with a parent occurs. Unfortunately, it is during the reunification period that fatal injuries are likely to transpire. We can only suppose that this occurs because of the stress of the re-adjustment on the part of both the child and the parent(s) without adequate counterbalancing support.

Economic Stress

Economic problems created by unemployment, drug and alcohol addiction, divorce, and out-of-wedlock births create stress in families. National studies of child abuse have cited economic stress as a major factor in child maltreatment.

Researchers studying child abuse suggest several ways to deal with the issue of children living in troubled homes. One way is to protect children from harm, but to do so without interfering. Another way is to be an advocate for grandchildren, but without engaging in conflict with parents. These suggestions are very difficult to follow. A later chapter of the book will give suggestions on intervening without causing alienation.

Blameless Problems

Rossi and Rossi, researchers of human bonding, found that when families experience difficulties over which they have no control - such as sickness, job loss, or death – they tend to draw close. Grandparents usually stand ready to help; they believe by doing so, they assist their adult children in becoming independent.

Patricia Perkins Slorah, Ph.D.

In contrast, emotional troubles (such as drug or alcohol problems, mental illness or child abuse) tend to cause schisms in families. Such problems tend to make adults dependent in an unhealthy way.

Special Issues in Divorce

Divorce, and the resultant changes that occur, can have a complex effect on families. Colleen Leahy Johnson researched this issue for a number of years and found that divorce brought maternal grandparents closer to their grandchildren and adult daughters, while remarriage sometimes caused problems after this closeness developed.

I have known grandparents who bought houses or condominiums for their divorced daughter and her children. When a boyfriend moved in, they controlled the use of space and, in some instances, crowded minor children out of their own home.

74

Family Intervention

Dr. Arthur Kornhaber, mentioned earlier in the book, has worked for many years to strengthen ties between grandchildren and grandparents. His research found that grandparents who criticize their grandchildren's caregiver or custodial parent were particularly at risk for being cut off from grandchildren. He advises grandparents to settle differences within the family without involving professionals.

Family Meetings. Dr. Kornhaber suggests that the adult generations agree on a time and a place for family meetings. An agenda should be developed to discuss the following points:

- Definition of the problem
- Causes of the problem
- Desirable outcome
- Possible options
- A mutually agreed upon plan
- Ways to carry out the plan
- Evaluation of the plan.

In America, all fifty states have laws that provide for court ordered resolution of grandparental estrangement, but these laws have serious defects. One defect is that they do not apply across state lines. Grandparents who obtained visitation in one state may have to petition in another state if the custodial parent moves to avoid the court order. A uniform federal grandparent visitation law is needed.

In the next chapter you will read the stories of several grandparents who were cut off from grandchildren. These stories are real, but the names have been changed to protect their identities as well as that of their grandchildren. These stories are typical of the situations discussed at support group meetings.

CHAPTER 9

GRANDPARENT STORIES

#1. Activist Grandmother

Anne Marie Hand is an attractive blond with large blue-green eyes. When she first contacted me, she had suffered the most devastating blow in her life. Without warning she was separated from her grandson, Douglas, whom she and her husband had reared for nine years. Deborah, their daughter, took Douglas bowling and at their expected time of return, only their daughter appeared. She told her parents she was taking him to live with her and they were no longer allowed to see Doug.

A New Life for Doug

A local counselor, well known to grandparents in similar situations, had been working with Deborah, for some time. This counselor has a reputation for routinely advising parents to separate caregiving grandparents and grandchildren without allowing them to say goodbye.

Consequently Douglas was taken from his friends, his school, and his church. His hair was cut, his sports activities were terminated, his clothing was left behind, and he was no longer allowed to have any contact with his grandparents.

As devastated as Anne Marie was, her husband – Deborah's father – was far worse. Everson suffered a stroke and massive heart attack, which his doctor said was brought on by the stress. They had changed their entire lives to raise Douglas, whom their daughter bore at the young age of sixteen. As a judge later stated, the Hands were rearing Deborah at the same time they were rearing her son.

Anne Marie is one of the most nurturing individuals I have ever met. Her entire life was devoted to giving Douglas an enriched life, even though she and Everson had few resources to spare.

Coping with Loss

In accordance with her nature, Anne Marie chose to start a grandparent support group. She also had several counseling sessions with a nationally known psychologist, Dr. Ruth Peters, who is supportive of caregiving grandparents in similar situations.

Additionally, through the Internet, Anne Marie became acquainted with a network of grandparents throughout the United States.

Through this network she made contact with a grandparent who lives in the same town to which Douglas had been taken by his mother and stepfather, Petros. This contact literally saved Anne Marie's sanity because the reports she received about her grandson's welfare indicated Douglas looked healthy and was doing well in school.

Unfinished Business

Still, like other grandparents in this situation, the Hands did not know what their daughter had told Douglas. They felt compelled to let their grandson know they loved him and had neither forsaken nor abandoned him.

Eventually, Anne Marie and Everson took the matter to court, but not before Deborah had married Petros and moved Douglas to another state over a thousand miles away. The legal costs, along with the travel costs to file in Douglas' home state, were difficult for the Hands.

The emotional costs of suing their daughter were even greater. There were scenes, tears, and accusations – reactions common to the situation. Nevertheless, the judge ruled in favor of the Hands and they were allowed to take Douglas out to lunch and on an overnight visit.

The time that I have known these grandparents spans eight years. To date they have had only one overnight visit with Douglas and this was at a hotel. From time to time he calls his grandmother while Deborah calls Anne Marie almost every day now, and sometimes talks for hours.

Deborah has tearfully apologized to Anne Marie several times over the telephone and is angry at the counselor, who advised her to change Douglas's life so suddenly and completely. Deborah has moved closer emotionally to Anne Marie, while Douglas has moved farther away.

At a family reunion recently, Douglas refused to look either of his grandparents in the eye and lets them know that his loyalties lie with Petros, which he appears to think precludes a close relationship with his grandparents. Anne Marie and Everson are puzzled by this because they have always believed they had a good relationship with Petros. Although Douglas has not said so, the Hands believe his stepfather does not want him to resume a relationship with them and consequently Douglas is unsure how to act around them.

Trouble Ahead for Deborah and Doug?

Doug's room at the Hand's home remains as he left it eight years ago. Even though now 17 years old and interested in girls, he told Anne Marie he wants nothing changed in his old room - a room designed for a nine-year-old boy.

Deborah is so caught up in her own life that she is unaware of the issues that Douglas will have to sort out as he matures. While this story may not appear to have a happy ending, I am predicting that Doug will turn to his grandparents as he struggles with the developmental issues in his past.

I believe they will gently guide him to accept the fact that both his grandparents and his mother love him. His grandparents did what they were asked to do and his mother did what she thought was the right thing to do at the time. I am confident that Douglas will sort it all out and know that he has always been loved and nurtured.

#2. They Gave up their Security

Bell and Bat Masterson are conservative, Catholic, southwesterners. Bat is a retired career military officer and Bell is a career homemaker. They are a delightful couple, whom I have known since 1989. Both are upbeat with lots and lots of energy.

They have two adult daughters – one who has been an absolute delight and the other, Mary Martha, has been the source of a great deal of heartache. Mary Martha is the mother of the Masterson's two grandsons, Murph (Murphy) and Sam (Samuel).

Problems Ahead

Mary Martha married young and against her parent's wishes. The marriage ended in divorce, three years and two children later. Although Bat and Bell are fond of their grandsons' father and are now closer to him than they are to Mary Martha, they knew the young lovers were too immature to make the marriage work.

After the divorce, the Mastersons moved Mary Martha, Murph and Sam in with them and financed her degree in Education. They did this with the idea that Mary Martha would be able to support herself and her children and eventually be able to afford her own home.

Putting Mary Martha through college proved to be a major problem since she was more interested in the opposite sex than in her studies. At one point she took out a student loan, dropped out of school, took the two children and moved with a taxi driver to South Carolina. It was unclear why she did this since she had no income and neither did her boyfriend.

Providing a Safe Haven

After about seven weeks Murph called their grandparents saying that they were out of money and food. Bat and Bell came to their rescue and moved them all back to Texas, which proved costly because their daughter had also moved her furniture to South Carolina.

Early on in their lives, Mary Martha began to use the boys to obtain money from her parents and her former husband. If they did not agree to her demands, she refused to let them see the boys.

Although Bat and Bell realized what she was doing, it was hard not to give in because Mary Martha was a neglectful mother. She took her sons to live in dirty, insect-infested housing in unsafe neighborhoods, and as preschoolers left her sons alone at night while she went out partying.

The Mastersons lived from crisis to crisis – a pattern that is familiar to grandparents in such situations. When problems became overwhelming, the boys would call their grandparents for assistance. One time Bell and Bat did not arrive fast enough and Murph's mother pulled out a handful of his hair, leaving a huge bald spot.

Polite, yet cool, Relationship

They had on-going family feuds; at one point Mary Martha took out a restraining order against the Mastersons (after she had moved out of their house). The Masterson's responded by successfully seeking court-ordered visitation. Now, they have a cool, reserved relationship: no open warfare, but very little contact. If they happen to meet in public, they are polite but nothing more.

Because Bat is retired he has been able to spend a great deal of time with the boys as they have matured. He has taught them ethics and positive values. It has not been easy because the boys for years had lived in a chaotic, permissive household.

Since her second marriage, Mary Martha has lost interest in holding the boys hostage. Their stepfather is a wonderful man who makes every effort to accommodate the boys since Sam and Murph rarely see their father, who spends most of his time out of the country.

Financial Sacrifices

Bell and Bat have exhausted their savings educating the boys in private Catholic schools, keeping them busy through travel and involvement in sports, and taking up the slack when their father had lapses of months without paying child support.

Bat was truly gratified when Murph wrote a school essay about him entitled, "The Man I Admire Most." Murph is away at school now, but keeps in touch often. Sam currently lives with his mother, but has 'Graham' as he calls Bell, do his weekly laundry. Sam and Bat go to out to dinner every Monday night and he and his grandmother spend one evening a week together at home.

The boys originally called Bell, 'Granny', but the nickname 'Graham' came about after a camping trip. The four of them sat around the campfire one night eating Smores. On the way to bed, Murph gave Bell a big hug and said, "I'm going to call you 'Graham' cause you're wonderful – just like Smores.

Bell specializes in providing comfort. Her cooking repertoire consists of the boys' favorite foods. They especially like chocolate cake, grilled cheese sandwiches, and oatmeal.

I remember the first time I met her in person after talking with her on the telephone for several years. She flew to meet me in Kansas City for a grandparent conference, where we shared a room.

I am not a good traveler and was quite sick after arriving at the hotel. There was a reception scheduled for late afternoon and I just could not make it. Knowing Bell's caring personality, I expected that she would bring me a snack from the party, although neither of us mentioned it.

Sure enough, Bell returned with a tray laden with stemmed glasses, china, and all sorts of goodies. When I laughed at the sight of her, she said hotel personnel had given her a hard time taking the tray out of the reception area, but she had prevailed.

Bell has suffered physically as a result of all the stress. During an especially difficult time she had an accident with her car. While she was outside the car, it became knocked out of gear with the motor running. This occurred in a crowded parking lot, so when the car began rolling in reverse, Bell, who weighs 105 pounds soaking wet, tried to stop it and was run over by her own car! She spent five days in the hospital and will suffer recurring pain due to her injuries.

Has it been worth it? You bet it has! Both boys are straight 'A' students and have received numerous academic awards. Both have jobs to earn spending money and neither has been in serious trouble. Both Murph and Sam close each contact with their grandparents with "I love you."

Once, Sam ended a telephone conversation with his French teacher (who reminds him of Bell) with "I love you" and was so embarrassed he didn't know what to do. He called his grandmother for advice, and was reassured his teacher surely thought 'how lucky Bell Masterson is to have such a loving grandson.'

Would things have turned out differently for these young men if their grandparents had not made them their first priority? Bat and Bell believe they would have. They hope and pray that their grandsons continue on the same path as they struggle to find their own place in the world.

#3. Bereaved Grandparent

My initial interview with Kathy took place in a small duplex in the commercial area out of which she conducts her business. As we talked, she played a tape of new-age music in the background, which gave a sort of surreal perspective to our dialogue.

Kathy, a platinum-blond with natural curls, is quite attractive and speaks articulately. During the year and a half she attended support group meetings; Kathy used the group for emotional support as well as for information as she struggled to maintain a relationship with her only grandchild, Taylor.

Kathy's daughter, Kay, was killed in a pedestrian accident when Taylor was just a toddler, so Kathy had to deal with both the shock of Kay's death as well as the loss of her grandson. Shortly after the death of her daughter, she lost her grandson to a man who was known to be physically abusive. The resultant distress was almost more than she could bear.

Kathy has had many problems with the baby's father. At one point, Rick had taken the baby and fled after physically assaulting Kay. Kathy initially tried to find the baby through the child welfare system, but later hired a private detective who determined the baby's whereabouts. Kathy also paid the legal expenses so her daughter could divorce Rick and regain custody of the child.

When her daughter died, Kathy's attorney told her that she could legally take the baby to Florida and file for custody of him there. However, at the airport, Rick and his friends wrested the baby from her arms and accosted Kathy. She possessed paperwork giving her the right to take the baby, but didn't have it with her at the airport.

When she returned to Florida after her daughter's death, Kathy went to bed for three months. She related that she was in terrible physical, emotional, and mental pain. The pain of losing her only daughter was compounded and dwarfed by having to hand over her grandson to a parent whom the detective she hired told her was a cocaine addict and alcoholic.

Finally taking matters into her own hands, with the assistance of an attorney friend and a grandmother in our support group, she wrote a letter to the judge describing the loss of her daughter and the difficulty she experienced in obtaining a court date for her visitation hearing. Surprisingly, the judge obliged her by setting a date for a hearing. In my experience with estranged grandparents, I had never heard of anyone filing a court petition without a lawyer, much less being granted a hearing before the judge.

Kathy had accomplished what the attorney and child protective services could not. When Kathy appeared before the judge, after persevering through two years of dealing with the state welfare system and the courts in Florida and Nevada, the judge asked her, "Where have you been for two years?"

After hearing Kathy's case, the judge awarded visitation with her grandson for two weeks every summer in the town in which he resides. Kathy initially did not have overnight privileges, which meant she had to return the child to his home every evening, however later she was granted the right to fly him to Florida for their visits. She was also given the right to telephone and send gifts and letters to him.

Kathy still considers it a mistake to have become involved with the child welfare system. In her view they did nothing to protect her grandson and only added to the delays in which she became embroiled in her quest for grandparental rights.

Kathy reported that she did not want to rear the child:

> I just want to see that he's being raised by somebody decent. He's not safe now. The bottom line is that I got three attorneys out there before it was over. It took actually two years and it wasn't until I contacted you at Grandparents' Rights and then I told you I'm going to write the judge [that I got to see the child]. That this violent man could keep my grandson

from me for two years – I don't
know what's happening.

Because his father told him that Kathy was responsible for his mother's death and that she stole all his toys, Doug is afraid to be open with her on their annual visits. While Kathy does not see indication of physical abuse, there is strong evidence of emotional abuse and she fears for him. When she appeared in court, the judge revealed to her that her former son-in-law's family is well known to local law enforcement officers.

Kathy has spent a great deal of money trying to protect the child and it has taken its toll on her meager resources. She feels, however, that it was worth it to be able to maintain her ties to her only grandchild.

Recently I spoke with Kathy on the telephone and she told me that her grandson is now 16 years old and their relationship is less than satisfactory. She reaches out to him, but he is very reserved toward her. She sends him cards and letters, yet does not receive replies. One Christmas she bought him a computer so they could exchange e-mail. When she does receive e-mail, it is from his father and stepmother. Kathy believes they feel remorseful about the events that occurred early in the child's life.

While this story does not – at this time – have a happy ending, I believe the situation will improve when Kathy's grandson turns 18. Rick has related to Kathy that he would like for Doug to attend college in Florida and that just might be the catalyst to re-establish the close relationship Kathy once enjoyed with her grandson.

#4. Grandparents Who Sacrificed Everything

In the spring of 1993 I traveled to a small, inland city in the middle of the state to interview Debbie Markson in a mobile home park on the outskirts of town where she lives with her husband, Rick. Debbie and Rick have had to give up their dream home in the country complete with swimming pool, and Rick has had to come out of retirement into a full-time job in order to pay arrears legal fees that they incurred in the fight to retain custody of Debbie's grandson, Joseph.

I initially met Debbie in 1991, shortly after she lost custody of her nine-year-old grandson, Joseph, whom she reared for over half his life. Her fight to preserve ties with Joseph nearly destroyed Debbie and her husband, Rick, who had a massive heart attack and, even though he is not legally related to Joseph, very nearly lost his life. It cost them their financial security and took several years to pay off the twenty-five thousand dollar legal bill they incurred in the lengthy court battle.

Debbie and Rick have suffered many hardships in their efforts to regain guardianship of Joseph, who spent four-and-a-half years with Debbie and Rick. Debbie has told me they would have gladly returned him to his parents if they had been capable of caring for him properly, but Debbie and Rick do not believe that the child's parents have ever been good parents to Joseph.

Child protective services in Ohio intervened on Joseph's behalf when he was an infant (in

1984) because he was severely battered. He spent a month in the hospital and nearly died. At the time Joseph was given back to his parents, Debbie had no rights to visitation because his parents were still married to each other. It was only through the efforts of an astute and caring attorney that rights were granted through the stepfather, Rick.

Although Joseph's mother, Nancy, is neglectful of him and his sister, it was Debbie's son, David, was the perpetrator of the abuse against Joseph, and he remains a peripheral figure in Joseph's life. Debbie does not make excuses for her son, but explains that she had reared five children alone after a divorce, and David was especially hurt when his father left. David used to cry himself to sleep after the divorce and call out for his father.

Debbie believes that this trauma probably stunted her son's emotional growth. His immaturity as an adult resulted in his lashing out at Joseph in an attempt to stop him from crying. He continues to pay child support every month for Joseph, but would willingly relinquish the responsibility if Joseph's stepfather would adopt him. Debbie is very angry at her son for his disinterest and constantly worries about Joseph's well-being. She said:

> It's going to cost hundreds of dollars to straighten him out – if ever. I told my husband if something isn't done, if she doesn't wake up, in a couple of years that child is going to be a juvenile delinquent and whose fault is it? [Cries softly.]

> He has become more than she can handle. When she got to the point that she couldn't control him, she put him in counseling. He ran away from home twice and said he was coming back down here. He refuses to do anything she says and he screams bites, kicks, spits, throws things, and knocks holes in the walls.

> I'm just so worried about him…What bother me the most is his anger outbursts.

Debbie does everything she can to help Joseph. When they visit him during the winter, she talks to his teachers and his guidance counselor. The lunch room manager at the elementary school told her they will not give Joseph hot lunches anymore, because his mother will not pay the money she owes. To keep him from running away, Debbie tries to get help for him from local child welfare authorities, which, she says, are less than cooperative most of the time.

Debbie and Rick continue to incur legal expenses because Joseph's mother refuses to let him come on annual visits to his grandparents with whom he wants to live. As a result Debbie must hire a lawyer every year to file a petition for the court-ordered visitation they were granted several years ago.

Joseph's well-being comes first with Debbie, and she will do whatever she has to do to make sure he is protected and cared for. The cost of caring has come high, and she and Rick have made many sacrifices. One luxury she has had to forego is money for her weekly visits to the beauty shop because Joseph regularly asks her to buy his clothes and shoes, which he badly needs. Debbie also tries to be available if he telephones for help. She says she used to be afraid to leave the house for fear she would miss Joseph's calls, but now feels confident that he will call again if he needs her.

I met Joseph a couple of years ago at a grandparents' support group meeting and I will never forget the look on his face as he gazed up at me. He had such a look of gratitude that to this day recalling this brings tears to my eyes. When I was in Crystal River interviewing his grandmother, his grandfather took him fishing so we could talk in private. While I was there, Joseph called and asked if he could see me because, as he explained to his grandmother, "She's for grandparents' rights."

Joseph as an Adult

Recently I spoke with Debbie on the telephone and she gave me an update on Joseph. Although he has had some problems during his teen years due to the anger he felt after being forced from his grandparents' home, he is now married and settled down. Debbie reports that he has no contact with his father and is considering petitioning the court for custody of his sister who still resides with their mother. Debbie, at last, feels at ease about Joseph and is confident that he is well on his way toward a happy, productive adult life.

#5 A Tale of Two Stories

Elizabeth's Story. Of all the narratives, Elizabeth Staunton's story most dramatically illustrates the random nature of grandparental estrangement and crack cocaine addiction. My experience with the Stauntons brought home to me, as no amount of study had done, the indiscriminate nature of crack cocaine addiction.

When I arrived at the Staunton home, I immediately felt a sense of peace in the lovely secluded home, filled with antiques and surrounded by lush Florida vegetation. The calming stillness was unbroken save for the ticking of the mantel clocks and our voices as the chronicle began to unfold.

These sights and sounds are a far cry from those most commonly thought to be associated with people involved with crack cocaine. The sounds of police and ambulance sirens wailing, the sight of broken glass, rundown housing and homeless men sleeping in doorways are usually thought of as the setting for crack addicts.

However, crack cocaine is different from any other powerful street drug, because it can be smoked. Therefore, people who wouldn't consider injecting drugs, use it – yet its effect is just as deadly. The craving that crack produces is different from, and more powerful than, any other street drug. Thus, the addict is likely to do almost anything to obtain the money for the next dose or 'fix.'

Elizabeth's forty-year-old daughter, Laura, who had just been released from community control, was also present for the interview. Laura, a graduate school study, is strikingly pretty and anyone meeting her for the first time would find it hard to believe that twice she had served time in jail for criminal activities associated with her crack cocaine addiction.

Laura told me that she had never been associated with the cocaine scene in high school or college; yet, when she was in her late thirties, crack wrecked her life in a very short time. Later in this chapter Laura relates the story of her addiction and the subsequent loss of custody of her children.

Elizabeth Staunton is a soft-spoken woman in her mid- sixties who had been caretaker for her three grandchildren for a period of time, when their divorced mother, who had custody was arrested for drug associated activities. During the children's stay, Elizabeth devoted herself to them. She took them to the beach (though born in Florida they had never been) and to Disney World. She paid for Tae Kwon Do and clogging lessons, and enrolled them in church and scouting activities.

Elizabeth began to suffer from the strain of caring for three children aged twelve, eleven, and ten. Her age and her husband's poor health increased the burden. In desperation she contacted the children's father, who had not seen them in three years, with the hope that he would assume part of the responsibility for them.

Instead, the father tried to turn the children against Elizabeth and his former wife, Laura, and eventually took them out of the state in defiance of the terms of the divorce decree. Although relations with her former son-in-law were strained, Elizabeth was able to see her grandchildren for a while after they went to live with their father. Then, suddenly, the children disappeared.

Just prior to their disappearance, their father had reported to the police that the family cat had been decapitated and left in the yard – a fact he associated with death threats he had allegedly received from criminals, whom he claimed are friends of Laura's. Laura showed me a copy of the police report and it was the opinion of the officer who answered the call, that the family dog had killed the cat.

Neither she nor her mother has any idea why Laura's former husband would abduct the children. They believe it is somehow connected with Laura's release from jail, and her attempt to contact them. Because Laura still does not understand his actions or the motives behind them, she worries that he may retaliate against her if she tries to locate the children.

At present Laura's record renders her vulnerable to any charges her former husband may file against her. If he accuses her of anything, regardless of whether there is any basis for it, she will be arrested and it will be up to her to prove her innocence. Therefore, Laura and her parents feel they must be very careful in the way they handle the situation.

Through tracing the automobile (using the registration number) that Laura's former husband stole, the Stauntons have located the children in another state. They know where the children are living and have friends checking on them. Both Laura and her mother intend to bring charges against the father after Laura has paid her debt to society.

Neither Laura nor Elizabeth believes that the children's father would maltreat the children, but there is reason for skepticism. Laura's former husband has broken a number of laws by taking the children out of the state, but so far has maintained the fiction that he still resides in Florida and he receives mail at his former Florida residence. His current wife's parents own this house and they illegally forward his mail, including the monthly welfare checks for the three children.

The interview with Laura and Elizabeth ended as I wish all grandparent stories involving adult children would – with both of them walking arm-in-arm to my car. When I first met Elizabeth she felt little hope for reconciliation with Laura, who had recently gone back to jail for violating her probation. The bitterness both felt toward each other has been replaced with gratitude. Elizabeth is grateful to have her daughter back and Laura is grateful to her mother for caring for her children. Both express optimism for the future.

Laura's Story. Laura's decline into crack cocaine addiction began with her marriage to a man with serious emotional problems, and was compounded by the birth of a child with a difficult-to-treat neuromuscular disease. The symptoms of his illness made it difficult for him to sleep, and the medication for this condition was hard to tolerate because of its side effects. His birth was closely followed by the births of two other children.

Laura did not work outside the home after the birth of the first child. She tried to compensate for her husband's increasing dysfunction and, at the same time, meet the needs of three small children. It became too much for her and resulted in a depression for which she sought help from her husband's psychiatrist.

Her husband, who was taking valium prescribed by his doctor, began to sniff Freon which he would obtain through the refrigeration company where he worked. This eventually resulted in his being diagnosed as permanently disabled and qualified for a government pension. Despite this fact, he continued to obtain Freon and eventually Laura was forced to have him committed to a mental hospital under the Baker Act.

During her husband's hospitalization, Laura decided there was no hope for their marriage. She filed papers for divorce, and informed her husband's extended family, who took him in upon his release from the hospital. After the divorce Laura was no longer able to afford her own psychiatric visits. The doctor, subsequently, cut off her prescriptions for Dexedrine which he had prescribed for depression – without allowing a gradual withdrawal from the drug.

The combination of coping with her son's illness, as well as the needs of two other young children, the divorce, and the drug withdrawal, pushed Laura over the edge into dependency on cocaine. Within a short time (about six months), in order to buy the drug she had sold her spacious home, complete with antique furnishings, and stole jewelry and other valuable items from her parents. Her subsequent arrest came when she signed her name while pawning stolen merchandise.

At the outset of her addiction, Laura had willingly given her children to her parents. Moreover, she resisted any emotional support and refused to have anything to do with them until after her second arrest. After reconciling with her parents she told me how grateful she is that her parents took her children in and spared them the worst of her addiction. She now recognizes the burden her mother so willingly shouldered and expresses gratitude for the support the grandparents' group continues to provide for her mother.

At the end of the interview she told me she had experienced a religious conversion while she was still incarcerated that has made it possible for her to remain free from addictive drugs. At the present time, Laura is residing with her parents and has been released from community control. She is allowed to attend classes and continue work on her graduate degree. She looks forward to regaining her rights and the custody of her children.

Ten Years Later. I recently spoke with Elizabeth, who gave me an update on Laura and the children. Two of the children now live with Elizabeth, while the youngest child, who is seventeen, remains in school in Virginia. Laura, after seven years of maintaining a drug-free record, has finally obtained a job that utilizes her many talents. She frequently appears on local television, and gives talks about the agency for which she works in a managerial position.

The pivotal event in being reunited with the children came about through their stepmother, who had become acquainted with a man through the Internet and flew to Las Vegas, where they were eventually married. The day she left, the oldest child called his grandmother and said he wanted to come home.

The children have related chilling stories about the abuse they suffered at the hands of their stepmother, which their father was either too ill, or disinterested to stop. They all said they were too afraid to call their grandparents, for fear their stepmother would somehow find out, and they would suffer retribution.

The oldest child outgrew his neuromuscular condition around the time he entered puberty, which may have had some impact on his decision to become a medical doctor. He is now in a pre-medical program and has maintained a 4.0 average. Because he made the highest grade ever recorded on a particular test at the university, he is being honored at an awards ceremony in the next few weeks. He worries about having the proper clothing to wear since he has never owned a suit.

Elizabeth reports that none of the children has been in any trouble and, so far, none has experimented with drugs. The only sad note to our conversation was the death of her husband who had fought Parkinson's disease for 29 years and finally succumbed to inherent complications. Elizabeth is grateful she was able to care for him without ever having to place him in a nursing home.

This story points up two important facts. One is the need for grandparents always to be ready for grandchildren to return; even though it may not always seem so, children know when they are loved by their grandparents. The second is that we should not underestimate the power that parents (or parent-figures) have over under-age children.

#6 Misunderstood Grandmother

Armandine and her daughter-in-law, Nedra, could not be more different. Armandine is an 82-year-old woman with a somewhat stately presence. She wears her hair in braids wrapped around her head, rather in the manner of a coronet. Her voice is deep and melodious, her elocution is perfect and her vocabulary extensive.

Nedra, by contrast, is wispy and rather evanescent. She gives the impression that while she may be bodily present, her thoughts are elsewhere, and at any moment she may disappear. Nedra has an artistic nature and does not like confrontation. Armandine, on the other hand, is used to managing large numbers of employees, and enjoys the challenge of working through differences.

Yet, these two people are very close: bound together by two small girls - Nedra's daughters who are Armandine's grandchildren. However, the relationship was not always so harmonious; five years ago, Armandine sued Nedra for grandparents' visitation.

Both women suffered the loss of a loved one - Nedra's husband, who is Armandine's son. A number of misunderstandings occurred surrounding the death, including conflict over the funeral and distribution of family heirlooms. While these disputes were brought about by other family members, and did not directly involve Armandine and Nedra, they caused both women added stress.

Armandine had been deeply involved in her son's affairs the last few months of his life and Nedra had resented this. Boundaries were crossed and misunderstandings resulted. Soon after the funeral Nedra heard that Armandine was planning to sue for custody of the children.

Because she could not understand why her daughter-in-law turned against her, Armandine sought information and emotional assistance from the grandparent support group. It was only after she had filed papers for visitation rights and the two went into mediation that Armandine discovered Nedra's fears about a custody battle for the children.

Steps to Resolution

The mediation agreement gave Armandine limited visitation with a gradual increase in duration and decrease in restrictions. At first the visits took place at a restaurant, and later the children, along with their mother, came to Armandine's apartment. In time, the visits were expanded to overnight visits. The mediator wisely provided a chance for the family to heal.

Both women have come to respect and like each other; Armandine admires Nedra and says she is an excellent mother. Armandine now has lung cancer and her daughter-in-law has been wonderful to assist her with the many tasks associated with her condition. Nedra even chose to spend her birthday at her mother-in-law's apartment.

Armandine is so grateful for her life now and gives credit to the support group for helping her turn things around. Resolving this conflict is an important developmental task for Armandine as she approaches the end of her life. Although she cannot leave her grandchildren a legacy of money, she can leave them with memories.

Armandine cherishes every minute she spends with the children. When they are apart, she busies herself making extensive scrapbooks for them. Each child will know who her ancestors were and something about the contribution they made to society.

Perhaps when they are older, and leaf through the pages their grandmother so lovingly assembled, they will be moved to think about their future. They will have to struggle as every young person must, to establish their own identity and set priorities for their life work, however, they will know where they came from, and maybe that will help them decide where they want to go.

CHAPTER 10

STEPS TO GRANDPARENTS' VISITATION

Pro Se. In Florida, grandparents can represent themselves to request court-ordered visitation; however to do so, you must use a visitation petition form that is similar to the one in APPENDIX D from the Clerk of the Circuit Court's office. Since the form in this book is for informational purposes only, you will need to obtain a form at the court house in the county *in which your grandchild resides*. The document will need to be notarized and if not prepared by a lawyer, the form must be signed by the individual who helped you fill it out.

This form is free; however, it could cost as much as several hundred dollars to file the petition with the court. As of this writing (in Florida), if the petition is admitted to the court, grandparents and the opposing parent are remanded to mediation, where they each split the cost of the mediation service.

If one party refuses to participate or an agreement cannot be reached, the petition is given to a judge to decide. This is a situation in which it may be important to have a lawyer represent your interests, although grandparents have prevailed without legal council. Many of the grandparents whose stories appear in this book obtained visitation without utilizing an attorney, however you must consider several questions such as: 1) Will you have strong opposition from the both parents?, 2) Is the child in serious danger?, 3) Does a parent already have court-ordered visitation with this child?

In APPENDIX B you will find Florida's grandparents' rights law in its entirety, which is similar to other state laws but varies in the circumstances in which the court will consider a petition. You will note that in Florida, as of this writing, grandparents whose adult child (the parent of the grandchild) has died do not have standing to request visitation, although most other states allow petitions in this instance.

APPENDIX E contains web sites that will provide you with the circumstances allowed in each state. Because these laws are constantly changing, I did not include a list of them in this book, but by referring to these sites you will obtain up-to-the-minute information.

Attorneys. Arguably, the best way to obtain any rights through the court system is to employ a lawyer. Look for one with a favorable rating in Martindale Hubbell (the highest rating is AV). This resource can be found at your local library or you can find it on the Internet – the address is under APPENDIX E: HELPFUL WEB SITES. You will be most successful using this web site if you have the attorney's firm name or law school from which he or she graduated. Otherwise, seek a referral for an attorney from a trusted friend. I do not advocate looking in the yellow pages of the telephone book for an attorney.

Many grandparents, however, are unable to afford such an expense. If you are a retiree living on a fixed income, the chances are high that you will not have extra money to spend on legal services. If you are no longer working, you will be unable to replace the thousands of dollars that litigation with a number of complications could cost.

If you cannot afford legal assistance, the information in this book will start you on your way toward obtaining your rights with very little capital outlay. If you are able to afford the services of an attorney, material contained in this book should insure that you will win in court and participation in a grandparent support group will help you with the emotional support necessary to tackle this issue on your own.

Grandparents most Likely to Prevail

You are most likely to gain visitation if you exhibit tact in all your dealings with the parents at issue. Attempt to be helpful and in all instances refrain from making accusations about the parents. Sometimes this requires great restraint, but worth it in the long run.

Conciliatory Stance. Judges are most likely to grant visitation to grandparents who are *cooperative*.

There are many emotionally laden situations in court-ordered visitation. Parents, who do not wish their children to have contact with grandparents, are likely to present a number of obstacles to visitation. For example, they may call at the last minute and say the child is unavailable, or conversely they may not call, and no one will be home when the scheduled visit is to take place. Parents may complain that the child is tired, cranky, and dirty after visits.

You may be required to provide all transportation or to include other children in the visitation. Children may be prevented from receiving mail or being told of phone calls from you. Grandparents have even told me of parents removing the tags, on Christmas and birthday gifts and telling their child that the presents were from them. You cannot react in anger to such provocations. To do so places added pressure on the child and may result in loss of visitation rights.

Positive Attitude Toward Parents. A *positive attitude* toward the child's parents goes a long way toward convincing judges and mediators to grant visitation. Even though you may have supportable allegations of maltreatment, it is unwise to bring them up in court. A wise judge or mediator will be able to ferret out that information without your help.

When court-ordered visitation is granted, it is with the tacit acknowledgement that the presence of the grandparents is needed. To undermine that position by being openly hostile toward a parent is self-defeating. Likewise, it is injudicious for grandparents to say anything to the child that may be misunderstood when later repeated to the parents.

Keep in mind that children are often questioned by parents after such visits.

Note that Visitation can be Reversed

Remember - what is given by the court can also be taken away. I remember vividly a grandmother calling to tell me that she had won contact with her grandchild after several years of court hearings. She was so elated that she became over-confident and called her former daughter-in-law to tell her in explicit terms what she thought of her. Unbeknownst to her, the child's mother was recording the conversation; and although it is not legally admissible in court, it was played for the judge, and consequently, her hard-won visitation was reversed.

Societal Changes put Children at Risk

Very few grandparents can turn their back on a baby or small child who is being put at risk for sickness, injury or death by the actions of that child's custodian. Do not risk alienating your grandchild's parents unless your grandchild is in immediate life-threatening danger. As you read throughout this book child abuse is occurring more frequently in American society.

By understanding the conditions that contribute to widespread child maltreatment, you most likely will feel less animosity toward the parents of children who may be at risk for abuse or neglect. Armed with this knowledge you are in a better position to protect your at-risk grandchild.

The point I am making is this - child maltreatment is epidemic, and it is often related to economic conditions which are beyond your control. What you can do is offer to baby sit, or buy the child what is needed, but keep such supplies at *your* house.

As grandparents, we are often the first to notice abuse and neglect. Yet, when we try to protect the children through the social service or legal system, we are likely to be branded as "baby snatchers" or "interfering parents who won't let go." Such allegations are not supported by fact.

Be Aware that State Laws are Tenuous

To make things even more difficult, state laws vary widely and are subject to change yearly. Just as grandparents have banded together to lobby for visitation rights, parents have organized to oppose them. If a particularly weak case of grandparents' rights is overturned by a higher court, that case can be used to eliminate similar cases from state law.

In Florida in 1996, grandparents lost the right to petition the court for visitation when an adult child died. This was due to the reversal of a case in which a grandparent won visitation after an adult child died. When the surviving parent appealed the judicial decision to grant visitation rights and won the appeal, not only did those particular grandparents lose their rights, but so did any other grandparents wishing to file a petition in the same situation in Florida.

Dorothy

Dorothy was one of those grandparents. She carefully saved enough money to hire an attorney and was thrilled when her petition for visitation was granted. Her elation was short lived, however, because her rights were reversed when new legislation took effect the day after a judge granted her the right to have regular visitation with her deceased son's only child. She now waits for the day the law will change so she can see her grandson.

While it may seem inconceivable that a parent could be so cruel, such circumstances are not uncommon. Young parents who have lost a spouse to death may want to turn their back on the pain and everything that reminds them of it; thus, they may remarry, sever existing connections, and bring "new" grandparents into their child's life.

Common Provisions in State Laws

State grandparent visitation laws are organized around the following categories:

- **Death.** Except in Florida, if a grandparent loses an adult child to death, that grandparent may petition the court for visitation with surviving grandchildren. Florida formerly allowed petitions in such cases, but no longer does so.

- **Divorce.** In an increasing number of states the parents of either the non-custodial parent (usually the father) or the custodial parent (usually the mother) may petition for visitation rights separate from those of the parent. In some states those rights are granted only at the time of the divorce; in other states they may be granted at any time after a divorce. *It is important to note that the petition* **must** *be filed* **BEFORE** *a stepparent adoption.*

- **Intact Families.** Florida had a provision that allowed grandparents to petition for visitation while the parents of their grandchild were still married to each other. Due to a State Supreme Court ruling, this provision was deleted from the state law. Check the AARP or the Grandparent Foundation website (APPENDIX E) for states in which such petitions are allowed.

- **Out-of-Wedlock Births.** Because these children are believed to be most likely at risk for abuse and neglect, grandparents who can prove legal ties can usually petition for visitation.

- **General Provision Clauses.** Some states have general provision clauses that do not stipulate the conditions under which grandparents may petition. Such states allow petitions that they believe have merit; courts grant or deny rights on the basis of each case.

Anyone May Need Grandparents' Rights

A bitter divorce, substance abuse, a sudden death, or any number of circumstances can put you, as a grandparent, at risk for losing touch with a grandchild. It is important to understand the complexity of the laws before you need to use them. When the unexpected occurs, you might react in the heat of the moment in ways that you will later regret. By reading this book, hopefully, you will be prepared to handle unfortunate circumstances in such a way that will not jeopardize your right to be a part of your grandchild's life.

In the previous chapters I have included stories of grandparents who fought for visitation with grandchildren in a variety of circumstances. The stories show how, through perseverance, many grandparents have prevailed. You may recognize situations with which your own children, your grandchildren, other family members, friends or neighbors are grappling.

You may have thought that such heartaches do not affect people who own their own home, have a job, are educated, and are well thought of in their community. You may have thought that such distress is reserved for people who are somehow at fault for their misfortunes. You are wrong. Everyone is at risk.

CHAPTER 11

TWELVE WAYS TO WIN

In the grandparent narratives throughout this book, you will notice commonalities. Everyone has to cope as best they can with generational difficulties and it is important that you recognize that these differences do not go away; this is an issue that will take a long time (if ever) to resolve. We are all rightfully concerned about the welfare of our grandchildren, and at first many of us mistakenly believed that if we could just be heard in court, everything would be fine.

For some, things worked out well; for others – like the Fredricksons – the results were disastrous. Many of us have criticized the custodians of the children, in hopes that we could change their behavior. The last thing we wanted to hear was "Be patient," we wanted changes now.

Through hearing other grandparent stories, we learned to keep a room ready for the children's return. We became convinced of the need to maintain calm in the face of provocation and many of us sustained stiff necks from keeping our chin up and turning the other cheek.

You may choose to reject some of the points below. If so, just forget about them for now. Later, you will probably come to accept them. If there were an easier way, believe me, I would have taken it! And remember, you don't have to like it, but you do have to follow these points if you want to win!

1. Try to Avoid Court

If you find it necessary to go to court, my suggestion would be to opt for mediation and work hard to make it successful. Judges are human beings who bring to the bench their individual biases. You cannot count on a hearing in front of a judge who is sympathetic to grandparents' rights.

Unfortunately, middle-class grandparents tend to have unrealistic expectations of the court system. Many of us erroneously believed that once we have our case before a judge, we would win easily, and we expected the judge to deal harshly with parents who withhold grandchildren from grandparents.

Unfortunately, many grandparents do not win in court and are often portrayed as meddlesome and interfering – even when the family situation clearly indicates a need for intervention.

2. Refrain from Criticizing

Children take it personally when someone they love is criticized. They feel that when anyone criticizes someone they love, they are being criticized. In effect, those who criticize either the child's parents or grandparents are doing just that.

Grandchildren are likely to side with those whom they see as being attacked. They are likely to love them all the more because of it. After all, they, too, have suffered because of the strife in the family, and the bond of suffering is a very powerful one.

3. Be Patient

Grandparenting in some circumstances is not trouble-free, but the rewards are great. You have the chance to be a good friend and guide to your grandchild as he or she makes the transitions from child to teenager to adult. Because of increased life expectancy for the first time in history, large numbers of grandparents will have the chance to know their grandchildren as adults.

With improved medical technology, some families now include five living generations. Older persons who practice reasonable health and safety measures can expect to live a long and productive life – longer and more productive than at any time in history.

4. Be Discreet when Reporting Maltreatment

When sexual abuse or severe physical abuse or neglect is suspected, child protective authorities should be notified. In Florida, CPS workers are supposed to investigate such cases within 48 hours, or sooner, if conditions are dire. *Grandparents should call the abuse hotline, which is listed in the telephone book, in order to be sure the complaint is registered.*

Although CPS personnel do not directly inform the parents of the person who made the complaint, they may give information which could reveal the identity of the abuse reporter. Do not volunteer the information that you called in a complaint; nothing good can come from this information. It is not necessary to lie about it – simply do not answer, or change the subject if you are asked directly.

5. Provide At-Risk Children a Haven

Children in situations where they are abused or neglected need a safe place to go. Grandparents should take such children in without being critical or condemning their parents. It is useless for nonprofessionals to attempt to change the behavior of another adult and it is foolish for parents of adult children to attempt this.

Several grandparents tell me they keep a supply of underwear, pajamas, and clean clothing at all times for younger children. For older children they keep shampoo, deodorant, and a blow dryer as they never know when the children will be dropped off – always with just the clothes on their back.

6. Forego Expensive Purchases

Grandparents of at-risk children may be inconvenienced and have to make sacrifices. It is important to get medical, nourishing food and adequate clothing for your grandchildren. Do not, however, make expensive purchases. Parents with drug or alcohol problems may sell these items in an attempt to obtain money to support their habit.

Grandparents have told me they cut the labels out of clothing they buy for grandchildren. They do this to keep parents from taking the clothing back to the store where it was purchased and exchanging it for articles for themselves.

7. Don't Lend Money You Cannot Afford

Before lending or giving money away, you should consider several points: 1) Can you afford to give money to your children now? How might that impact your security later on? Do not count on getting back money that you lend; it is far better to consider it a gift than to suffer rancor because it is not repaid.

2) After adult children receive money for a down payment on a house, a car, or anything else, they are unlikely to welcome advice on how to manage their finances. When parents perceive that they need to protect their "investment" by offering unsolicited advice, problems are likely to occur.

Too, when adult children depend on their parents to bail them out of financial disasters, they never develop the self-discipline to become independent adults. I have known several examples when such situations turned tragic. One occurrence comes to mind in which an adult son cut off all contact with his dying father because his father refused to cover any more bad checks his son had written. In another instance, an adult son committed suicide when his parents refused to put any more money into his failing business.

8. Be Reserved with Difficult Parents

The best way to get along with difficult family members is to treat them as you would a neighbor – use the same tact and reserve. Limit the amount of time you spend with them and keep

your expectations low. That way
you will be pleasantly surprised if
they are congenial. Do not,
however, count on that behavior
permanently. Carefully consider
the setting in which you will be
seeing them and have an escape
plan; that way you can exit
gracefully if things start to fall
apart.

9. Do Not Alienate Anyone with Power

It is unwise for grandparents to
engage in conflict with anyone
who has power over their
grandchildren. It is possible to be
concerned and helpful about
problems without jeopardizing
one's resources and family
solidarity. If you are already
embroiled in such a situation, seek
out a support group near your
home; if none exists apologize for
whatever is causing hard feelings

and attempt to smooth over difficulties.

10. Be Tactful When a Death Occurs

Your relationship with your grandchild in such a situation is going to hinge, to a large degree, on how well you get along with your grandchild's parent. He or she may well remarry, start another family, and move away. Many are anxious to put the pain of bereavement behind them and are not willing to be reminded of the painful past. Do not discuss the past with parents in this situation.

Do not upset your grandchild by talking about his or her deceased parent. If the child asks questions, answer them in an upbeat way. Tell them funny stories about something their parent did as a child. If you are sentimental, the child may become upset and react later when they return home. Be warned that parents have used such situations to discontinue visitation.

It will be up to you to make the effort to retain ties. Offer to let the family stay with you if they are in town and go out of your way to be friendly and helpful to all family members. You may not be able to spend all the time alone that you want with your grandchild because of your involvement with the family, but at least you will be able to retain ties that otherwise may be broken.

11. Be Judicious when Giving Gifts

Inquire before giving gifts that may not be acceptable to the grandchild's parent. If there are half-siblings living in the household, it may be advisable to give them small gifts at Christmas.

Don't give parents the idea that you are competing for the child's affection. If the parents give one dollar for each tooth that falls out, make sure you don't give more than that.

If there is a need for warm clothing or other necessities, don't take the child on expensive vacations. Rather, try to be useful and provide gifts that are not in conflict with the lifestyle of the parents.

12. Don't Put Your Grandchild in a Bind

Don't give your grandchild food or gifts you know parents don't want them to have. No matter how difficult the restrictions parents may impose, try to stay within their guidelines, unless of course, it would be harmful to the child. If you insist on doing things that the child knows his parent has disallowed, it will cause the child to feel uncomfortable.

Never Give Up

I realize the suggestions above are difficult to follow. Remember that I have been there and experienced the extreme frustration that you may now be feeling. Too, I have observed over the years the grandparents who chose to make their own path. Heartbreak follows doing what you want to do, rather than what you need to do.

When you follow the advice in this book, you will reap rewards. You may not have the relationship with your grandchild that you would like, but you will have gone a long way toward helping that child survive a very difficult situation.

Grandparenting is really about empowering our descendants. Many older people have told me they did not realize - at the time - the sacrifices their parents or grandparents were making for them. But they recognize the benefits they now enjoy because of those sacrifices. Your grandchildren are lucky to have someone who cares enough about them to overcome the hurdles you have encountered.

I know numerous grandparents who waited years for their grandchildren to seek them out. They continued to send cards at birthdays and holidays without ever hearing a single word. Others put birthday and Christmas gifts in a chest because they were forbidden to send them. They did this with the faith that someday they would be reunited.

Grandparents who did those things, that seemed so futile at the time, eventually were reunited with the grandchildren. Each unanswered card had been carefully kept – hidden away from parents – in a drawer. These children knew they were loved. What a wonderful gift to offer. Sometimes that is all we can give, and that is enough.

BIBLIOGRAPHY

Cherlin, A.J. & Furstenburg, F.F. (1986) *The New American Grandparent: A Place in the Family, A Life Apart*. New York: Basic Books.

Eisenberg, L. (1981) Cross-Cultural and Historical Perspectives on Child Abuse and Neglect. In *Child Abuse & Neglect*. Vol. 5: 299-308.

Elder, G. H., Modell, J., & Parke, R.D. (1993) Studying Children in a Changing World. *In Children in Time and Place: Developmental and Historical Insights*. New York: Cambridge University Press.

Finkelhor, D. & Korbin, J. (1988) Child Abuse as an International Issue. In *Child Abuse & Neglect.* Vol.12: 3-23.

Garbarino, J. & Gilliam, G. (1980) *Understanding Abusive Families*. Lexington, MA: Lexington Books.

Herst, C. with Padwa, L (1998) *Mothers of Difficult Daughters*. New York: Villard Books.

Johnson, C. (1988) *Ex Familia*. New Brunswick: Rutgers University Press.

Kingson, E., Hirshorn, B., & Cornman, J. (1986) *Ties That Bind*. The Gerontological Society of America. Cabin John, MD: Seven Locks Press.

Korbin, J.E. (1985) Fatal Maltreatment by Mothers: A Proposed Framework. In. *Child Abuse & Neglect.* Vol. 13: 481-489.

(1979) A Cross-Cultural Perspective on the Role of the Community in Child Abuse and Neglect. In *Child Abuse & Neglect.* Vol. 3: 9-18.

Kornhaber, A. (1986*). Between Parents and Grandparents*. New York: Berkley Books.

(2002) *The Grandparent Guide*. Chicago: Contemporary Books.

Kuhn, C., Swartzwelder, S., & Wilson, W. (1998) *Buzzed.* New York: W. W. Norton.

Margolin, L. (1992) Child Abuse by Mothers' Boyfriends: Why the Overrepresentation? In *Child Abuse & Neglect*, Vol.16: 541-551.

Minkler, M. & Roe, K. (1993) *Grandmothers as Caregivers: Raising Children of the Crack Cocaine Epidemic.* Newbury Park: Sage.

Moore, J. (1985) *The ABC of Child Abuse Work*. Brookfield, VT: Gower.

Rossi, A., & Rossi, P. (1990) *Of Human Bonding.* New York: Aldine de Gruyter.

Segal, E. & Karp, N. (1989) *Grandparent Visitation Disputes: A Legal Resource Manual*. Chicago: American Bar Association.

Shengold, L. (1999) *Soul Murder Revisited.* New Haven: Yale University.

Slorah, P. (1995) *Grandparents of Children at Risk for Abuse and Neglect.* Tampa: University of South Florida Dissertation in Applied Anthropology.

(1999) Evolution of Work and Family. Cutting Edge Column. In *American Anthropology Newsletter*, January.

(1998) Grandparents, Gray Power and Grassroots Organizing: Implications for Anthropologists. In *Practicing Anthropology*. Vol. 20: No. 2.

Sokolovsky, J. (1997) Bringing Culture Back Home: Aging, Ethnicity and Family Support. In *The Cultural Context of Aging*. Westport, Connecticut: Bergin & Garvey.

Sokolovsky, J. & Vesperi, M. (1991) The Cultural Context of Well-Being in Old Age. In *Generations*. Vol. XV (1): 21-24.

Strathern, M. (1992) *After Nature: English Kinship in the Late Twentieth Century.* New York: Cambridge University Press.

Terr, L. (1990) *Too Scared to Cry.* New York: Basic Books.

Wallerstein, J. (1984) Children of Divorce: Preliminary Report of a Ten-Year Follow-up of Young Children. In *American Journal of Orthopsychiatry* Vol. 54: 444-458.

Zimmerman, S. (1992) *Family Policies and Family Well-Being.* Newbury Park: Sage.

APPENDIX A: FREQUENTLY ASKED QUESTIONS

1. **What is court-ordered visitation?** It is a legal document issued by a judge and stating that visitation is to take place on certain dates for specific periods of time.

2. **What should I ask for in visitation?** Ask for the following specifics: how often visitation will occur, how long the visits will last, who is responsible for transporting the child, what holidays are included, if letters, telephone calls, and gifts are allowed and the frequency of each. Try to anticipate trouble spots and cover them by the judge's order.

3. **What if parents don't comply with court-ordered visitation?** They can be fined or put in jail.

4. **How can I find a grandchild who was taken out of state to avoid visitation?** Any specific information, such as the child or parent's Social Security number,

date of birth, license plate number, and drivers' license number can be helpful in finding them. You can also check with the post office for a forwarding address. Depending on your situation, you may have to engage the services of a licensed private investigator. If the parent is receiving any support money through a government agency, it should not be difficult to find them.

5. **How much is it going to cost me to engage a lawyer to obtain visitation?** Usually the initial consultation is free, but clarify that fact before setting the appointment. Better lawyers cost more, but if you cannot afford the fees you may be able to negotiate terms.

6. **What can I do if I can't afford a lawyer?** You can file your own petition. Contact the judge's secretary to notify the court that you will be representing yourself. Sometimes you can write your circumstances in a letter to the judge.

7. **How can I get a copy of my state's visitation law?** Look on the internet on

the web site for your state government. If you do not have access to a computer, call your state representative or senator and request a copy of the law.

APPENDIX B: A SAMPLE LAW

Chapter 752 Florida Statute on Grandparental Visitation Rights

752.001 Definitions

752.01 Action by grandparent for right of visitation; when petition shall be granted.

752.015 Mediation of visitation disputes.

752.02 Persons who must be served notice of petition; manner of service.

752.07 Effect of adoption of child by stepparent on right of visitation: when right may be terminated.

752.001 Definitions – For purposes of this chapter, the term "grandparents" shall include great-grandparents.

752.01 Action by grandparent for right of visitation; when petition shall be granted.

(1) The court shall, upon petition filed by a grandparent of a minor child, award

reasonable rights of visitation to the grandparent with respect to the child when it is in the best interest of the minor child if:

(a) ~~One or both parents are deceased;~~ (Amendment A was declared unconstitutional in 1998.)

(b) The marriage of the parents of the child has been dissolved;

(c) A parent of the child has deserted the child;

(d) The minor child was born out of wedlock and not later determined to be a child born within wedlock as provided in s.42.091; or

(e) ~~The minor is living with both natural parents who are still married to each other or there is a broken relationship between either or both parents of the minor child and the grandparents, and either or both parents have used their parental authority to prohibit a relationship between the minor child and the grandparents.~~ (Amendment E was declared unconstitutional in 1996.)

(2) In determining the best interest of the minor child, the court shall consider;

    (a) The willingness of the grandparent or grandparents to encourage a close relationship between the child and parent or parents.

    (b) The length and quality of the prior relationship between the child and the grandparent or grandparents.

    (c) The preference of the child if the child is determined to be of sufficient maturity to express a preference.

    (d) The mental and physical health of the child.

    (e) The mental and physical health of the grandparent(s).

    (f) Such other factors as are necessary in the particular circumstances.

(3) This act does not provide for grandparents' visitation rights for children placed for adoption under Chapter 63 except as provided in s. 752.07 with regard to adoption by a stepparent.

752.015 Mediation of visitation disputes.
Let it be the public policy of this state that, if families are unable to resolve their differences

regarding grandparental visitation, the families participate in formal or informal mediation services that may be available. When families are unable to resolve differences relating to grandparental visitation and a petition is filed pursuant to s. 752.01, the court shall, if such services are available in the circuit, refer the case to family mediation in accordance with rules promulgated by the Supreme Court.

752.02 Persons who must be served notice of petition; matter of service. – Notice of the filing and a copy of, the petition for grandparental visitation rights shall be served on the parents of the minor child in the manner prescribed by chapter 48.

752.07 Effect of adoption of child by stepparent on right of visitation; when right may be terminated. – When there is a remarriage of one of the natural parents of a minor child for whom visitation rights may be or have been granted to a grandparent pursuant to s. 752.01, any subsequent adoption by the stepparent will not terminate any grandparental rights. However, the court may determine that termination of such visitation rights is in the best interest of the child and rule accordingly, after affording the grandparent an opportunity to be heard.

Patricia Perkins Slorah, Ph.D.

APPENDIX C: FACTORS CONSIDERED BY THE COURT IN DETERMINING THE BEST INTEREST OF THE CHILD

- The love, affection and other emotional ties between grandparents and grandchild;

- The capacity and disposition of the parties to give the child love, affection, and guidance;

- The nature of the relationship between the petitioner and the grandchild and the desirability of maintaining that relationship;

- The moral fitness of the parties;

- The mental and physical health of the parties;

- The reasonable preference of the child, if the child is of sufficient age to express a preference;

- The willingness and ability of the petitioner to facilitate and encourage a close and continuing relationship between the child and the other parties;

- Any other factors which the court considers to be relevant to a just determination regarding visitation or access.

APPENDIX D: GRANDPARENTS' VISITATION PETITION FORM

INSTRUCTIONS FOR FLORIDA SUPREME COURT APPROVED FAMILY LAW FORM 12.984, PETITION FOR GRANDPARENT VISITATION

This form should be typed or printed in black ink. After completing this form, you should sign the form before a notary public. You should file the original with the clerk of the circuit court in the county where the child(ren) lives/live and keep a copy for your records.

For your case to proceed, you must properly notify the other party(ies) of the petition. If you know where he and/or she lives, you must use personal service. (For clarification of personal and constructive service, ask an employee of the clerk of the circuit court.) If you absolutely do not know where he/she lives, you may use constructive service. However, if constructive service is used, the court may grant only limited relief, if any. The law regarding constructive service is very complex and you may wish to consult an attorney regarding these issues.

If personal service is used, the respondent(s) has/have 20 days to answer after being served with your petition. Your case will then generally proceed in one of the following three ways:

DEFAULT. If after 20 days, no answer has been filed, you may file a Motion for Default, Florida Supreme Court Approved Family Law Form 12.922(a), with the clerk of court. Then, if you have filed all of the required papers, you may call the clerk, family law intake staff, or judicial assistant to set a final hearing. You must notify the other party(ies) of the hearing by using a Notice of Hearing (General), Florida Supreme Court Approved Family Law Form 12.923, or other appropriate notice of hearing form.

UNCONTESTED. If the respondent(s) file(s) an answer that agrees with everything in your petition or an answer and waiver, and you have filed all of the required papers, you may call the clerk, family law intake staff, or judicial assistant to set a final hearing. You must notify the other party(ies) of the hearing by using a Notice of Hearing (General) mentioned above.

CONTESTED. If the respondent(s) files(s) an answer that disagrees with or denies anything in your petition, and you are unable to settle the disputed issues, you should file a Notice for Trial, Florida Supreme Court Approved Family Law Form 12.924, after you have filed all of the required papers. Then you should contact the clerk, family law intake staff, or judicial assistant for instructions on how to set your case for trial (final hearing). Some circuits may require the completion of mediation before a finally hearing may be set.

Remember, a person who is not an attorney is called a nonlawyer. If a nonlawyer helps you fill out these forms, that person must give you a copy of a Disclosure from Nonlawyer Florida Family Law Rules of Procedure Form 12.900

(a), before he or she helps you. A nonlawyer helping you fill out these forms also must put his or her name, address, and telephone number on the bottom of the last page of every form he or she helps you complete.

IN THE CIRCUIT COURT OF THE _____

JUDICIAL CIRCUIT, IN AND FOR _____
_____COUNTY,
FLORIDA

Case No.: _____

Division: _____

_____,

_____
Grandparent (s),

And

_____

_____

Respondent(s).

PETITION FOR GRANDPARENT VISITATION

I/We, {full legal name(s)}_____

_____

_____ being
sworn, certify that the following information is
true:

1. This is a request for grandparent(s)
visitation, under chapter 752, Florida Statues.
2. The minor grandchild(ren) has (have) been
living in the State of Florida within the
jurisdiction of this Court.
3. I/We desire visitation with the following
minor grandchild(ren).

Name Birthdate   **Age**   **Sex**

_____

_____

_____

_____

_____

1. The ( ) mother, or ( ) father of my (our)
grandchild(ren) is my (our) ( ) son or ( )

daughter. A copy of my (our) child's (respondent's) birth certificate is attached.

2.[Check all that apply]

_____a. The mother and father of the grand(ren) are divorced.

_____b. The ( ) mother or ( ) father of the grandchild(ren) has (have) deserted the grandchild(ren).

_____c. The parents were not married when the grandchild(ren) was (were) born and did not marry after the grandchild(ren)'s birth, and paternity has been established.

1.I/We are requesting the following visitation: {explain} _____

_____

_____

_____

_____

2.It is in the best interests of the grandchild(ren) that the grandparent(s) be allowed reasonable rights of visitation with the grandchild(ren). This is in the grandchild(ren)'s best interests because: {explain}_____

Patricia Perkins Slorah, Ph.D.

_____

_____

_____

_____

_____

_____

I understand that I am swearing or affirming under oath to the truthfulness of the claims made in this petition and that the punishment for knowingly making a false statement includes fines and/or imprisonment.

Dated: _____

Signature of Grandparent_____

_____

Printed name: _____

Address: _____

City, State, Zip: _____

Telephone Number: _____

Fax Number: _____

STATE OF FLORIDA

COUNTY OF _____

Sworn to or affirmed and signed before me on

_____

By _____

_____

Notary Public or Deputy Clerk

_____

[Print, type, or stamp
commissioned name of
notary or clerk.]

_____ Personally known
_____ Produced
Identification

Type of identification
produced _____

_____

IF A NONLAWYER HELPED YOU FILL OUT THIS FORM, HE/SHE MUST FILL IN THE BLANKS BELOW: [FILL IN ALL BLANKS]

I, {FULL LEGAL NAME AND TRADE
NAME OF NONLAWYER} _____

Patricia Perkins Slorah, Ph.D.

_____

_____ a

nonlawyer, located at {street} _____

_____,

{city} _____, {state}

_____,

{phone} _____, helped {name} _____

_____, who is the (one of the)

petitioner(s), fill out this form.

THE ABOVE IS MEANT AS INFORMATIONAL ONLY. YOU MUST REQUEST A FORM FROM THE COURT IN THE STATE IN WHICH YOUR GRANDCHILD LIVES.

APPENDIX E: HELPFUL WEB SITES

www.grandparenting.org – Foundation on Grandparenting site. Contains current information on grandparent visitation laws in all 50 states.

www.aarp.com – American Association of Retired Persons' site. Chart of information on grandparent state laws.

www.grandparentsrights.org – Attorney Richard Victor's site with a variety of articles on the subject.

www.grandtimes.com – Articles on obtaining grandparents' rights.

www.martindale.com – Click on lawyer locator to find the rating of attorneys in your area.

ABOUT THE AUTHOR

Dr. Patricia Slorah is an early childhood educator, gerontologist and applied anthropologist. She taught young children for 12 years, and taught both undergraduate and graduate students at the University of South Florida in Tampa for five years.

Dr. Slorah has researched the issue of grandparents' rights for fourteen years and in the capacity of both grandparent and researcher appeared on local and national television (Good Morning America). She is considered an expert on the subject and has testified both at the national and state levels of government. She has been featured in newspapers across the country including the St. Petersburg Times, the Ft. Lauderdale Sun Sentinel, the Cleveland Plain Dealer, and the Wall Street Journal, as well as in the magazine Modern Maturity.

Dr. Slorah lives in Florida with her husband of 43 years, Jack; their granddaughter, Brittany; and great-granddaughter, Hailey. The Slorah's daughter, Michelle, lives in a nearby town with their 12-year-old grandson, Tyler.

Made in the USA
Lexington, KY
12 August 2015